The Works of Affonso Eduardo Reidy

Introduction by S. Giedion – Text by Klaus Franck

Frederick A. Praeger, Publishers, New York

BOOKS THAT MATTER

Introduction translated by Mary Hottinger
Text translated by D. Q. Stephenson, The English Institute, Basel

Published in the United States of America in 1960
by Frederick A. Praeger, Inc., Publishers
64 University Place, New York 3, N.Y.
© 1960 by Verlag Gerd Hatje, Stuttgart
Library of Congress catalog card number: 60–6997
Printed in Germany

Contents

Affonso Eduardo Reidy
and Contemporary Brazilian Architecture

In the last twenty or thirty years, new directions in contemporary architecture have not come from Europe alone. A universal civilization is approaching, and its development shows no symptoms of international standardization. Its common element is its conception of space, which is in keeping with both the emotional structure and the intellectual outlook of the period. It is not the individual, detachable form which is the universal factor in contemporary architecture, but the apprehension of the object in space, the conception of space. That holds true for all creative epochs, as it does for our own. The space-time concept, the way in which volumes are placed in space and establish mutual relationships, the way in which interior space is isolated from exterior space or openings are introduced to enable the two to interpenetrate — all these are common and fundamental elements in the architecture of our time.

There is yet another factor of equal importance, one that arises from an attitude shared by the best contemporary architects. These architects aim, above all, at taking full account of the changeless atmospheric and topographical conditions of a country, which are no longer obstacles but springboards for the creative imagination. It has often been observed that the painting of the present century has repeatedly taken soundings of the past in order to renew contact with kindred elements in mankind of earlier times and to derive strength from this contact. Neither in painting nor in architecture does this involve an imitation of forms, but rather a kinship of spirit.

I have elsewhere called this coming to terms with pre-existing atmospheric and topographical conditions a "new regionalism." The contemporary conception of space, the contemporary impulse to expression attempts a new synthesis with these timeless constants.

The way in which the new regionalism is handled by creative-minded architects depends entirely on the pre-existing problems and conditions, which vary from country to country. Within this common concept of space, many different forms of architecture are developing, leading to unexpected situations. In the Near East, for instance, the architect of today stands in a new relationship to building methods which are thousands of years old. In Egypt, he will renovate fellaheen villages with local materials, dried Nile mud, reeds, and so on — preserving the original plan of the house, in which men and animals share the living space, but abiding by the planning and principles of our day. A young American architect, trained at Harvard by Walter Gropius, attempted to apply the same method in the Cairo Ministry. It was received with nothing but misgivings. What was required of an American was "modern methods," the imitation of Western civilization as it is understood there, with the utilization of established regional conditions in a new sense.

This full acceptance of existing conditions, and their exploitation to obtain a more powerful architectonic expression, can also be observed in large public buildings. The "butterfly roof" of the High Court of Justice in Chandigarh is an instance of it; it is quite characteristic that Walter Gropius, in collaboration with a German sculptor, should have attempted to use the water of the Tigris to moderate the temperature in the University buildings in Baghdad, and that Alvar Aalto should design the Civic Center of Baghdad without an air-conditioning plant. On the other hand, in the same city, an architect schooled in the European decorative tradition introduced into his building all the technological paraphernalia of America; the only thing certain about it is that it will not work. Such individual diversity in architecture, with a common basis of fundamentals, represents one of the most hopeful aspects of the entire modern development.

Affonso Eduardo Reidy: His Personality

Affonso Eduardo Reidy was born in Paris in 1909. His father was English, his mother a Brazilian of Italian origin. In his architecture, Reidy is fully in line with the spirit of Brazilian developments, in which he plays his own personal part. He is an outstanding town planner. In his twenties, he was already working under Alfred Agache, the French town planner in vogue at the time, who, among other things, designed a large-scale plan for the city of Rio de Janeiro. In 1930, Lucio Costa, the most distinguished mind among the Brazilian architects, appointed Reidy assistant to Gregori Warchavchik at the National Academy of Fine Arts. Warchavchik was the first to counter the rise of international academic colonialism on Brazilian soil with a whiff of architectural modernism. Not long after, Affonso Reidy was appointed as full Professor to succeed Warchavchik.

In 1931, he shared (with another architect) the first prize in the competition for a hostel for homeless persons. "The Inn of Good Intentions," which was built according to his plans, already revealed the essentials of his style.

In 1936, Lucio Costa invited Reidy to work with the team of young architects who were designing the Ministry of Education and Health in Rio de Janeiro. It is with this building that Brazil took her place in the history of modern architecture. Le Corbusier was invited to act as consultant. He was more. It was he who gave the final impulse to Brazil. His influence can be seen in every detail: in the smooth, curving wall with the sculpture by Lipchitz (compare Le Corbusier's Swiss House at the Cité Universitaire, Paris, in 1935), in the use of adjustable sun-screens on the north façade as an important architectonic factor, in the pillars (over 30 ft. high for ventilation reasons), which immediately took their place as a permanent feature of Brazilian architecture.

Brazil was indeed ready for Le Corbusier, while a country like Argentina was not. There were young architects in Brazil who could profit by Le Corbusier's experience, insofar as was applicable to local conditions, and, while maintaining their own independence, could further develop it within their own new regionalism.

The next important step for Reidy came in 1947, when he became a member of the Department of Public Housing in Rio de Janeiro and designed the residential neighborhood of Pedregulho. For some time, this was the only residential housing plan. But others followed, and Pedregulho represented Reidy's entrance into architecture on the grand scale.

Reidy lacks the light hand and stimulating formal brilliance of Oscar Niemeyer. His imagination is more subdued. His buildings are almost forbidding. They must be conquered. Their quality can be felt at first glance, but each one of them requires a careful examination of the floor plans and of the equally varied organization of the different levels. The hand at work is subtle, transforming the simple product of a given situation and a set program into a work of art in much the same way as a master of language or form brings out the ultimate secrets hidden in his material.

The capricious contours of the Brazilian terrain are not obstacles; rather, they act as a stimulus to his imagination. His buildings are not placed on the ground — though they seem to grow out of it, to be a part of it, they are independent products of human creativity.

A similar principle governs the organization of his buildings, with a decisive relationship between interior and exterior space. At his present stage of development, there is no inevitable choice between a glass frontage or a windowless wall. Both are possible. But what is coming more and more to the fore is the opening — that is, the manner in which the wall is broken up. Modern architecture and sculpture both make use of the opening. In architecture, it is by no means restricted to vertical planes or to the elements of exterior walls, such as pillars or sun-screens, which, especially in Reidy's work, constantly reappear as constructive and formal elements and lend life to the vertical surface. An opening in the horizontal plane also enhances space. To a certain extent, it has always been a factor in Western architecture. But it was never possible before to cut away parts of ceilings or floors, opening vistas upward or downward and giving visual expression to the unity of interior and exterior space. Free rein must be given to the architectural imagination if the rigid surface of the various levels is to be treated as a malleable substance. The Brazilians — especially Oscar Niemeyer and Affonso Eduardo Reidy — have already made great strides in the use of openings on the horizontal plane. An example is Reidy's insurance office, Montepio dos Empregados Municipais, in Rio de Janeiro (1957). Once this kind of imagination has been awakened, it gives rise to fresh developments in which obstacles are converted into assets: the precipitous character of the Rio terrain provides a stimulus. In Reidy's work, we can see this principle operating in even the smallest dwelling house. The patio, or inner courtyard, of the house built for Carmen Portinho in Rio de Janeiro (1950—52) has openings to show the steep fall of the ground beneath. In the winding housing block at Pedregulho, which is raised on pillars, the terrain is exploited in such a way that the entrance is almost halfway up the block and leads to a second story on pillars. As far as this writer knows, this is the first instance of a double structure of pillars being used in a residential block.

Affonso Reidy's work consists mainly of large designs: theaters, museums, schools, blocks of offices, and the beginnings of urban planning which are so characteristic of him.

Theaters

A small popular theater built by the municipality in an industrial quarter of Rio de Janeiro (1950—51), set in a garden laid out by Burle-Marx, shows Reidy's skill in flexibility of modeling in its curved bench and in the heavy horizontal accent of its projecting eaves.

In comparison, his design for a students' theater in Rio de Janeiro (1955) is conceived more as a self-contained block.

Museums

The Museum of Visual Arts (1952), situated on one of the main streets of São Paulo, has the shape of a three-sided prism, with wide openings, a very free treatment of the three stories, and a winding perforation of the third-floor ceiling.

The Museum of Modern Art, beautifully situated on a beach at Rio de Janeiro, and combined with a theater and school, is a step toward an active artistic education of the public. The art collection is not isolated. The outlook on the sea lies open. The principle that exclusive overhead or lateral lighting should depend on the nature of the exhibits is fully acceptable, like the variation of large and small rooms which gives a maximum of spatial adaptability.

Schools

Of the various schools by Reidy, the experimental school in Paraguay (1953) is the most buoyant in treatment. The handling of the reinforced concrete is delicate and masterly. There is a rare harmony in the uniform orientation of the long rectangular building. The reinforced concrete frames of the school building, which stretch far outward, serve partly as protection against the sun and also facilitate the spatial perforation of the stories.

Office Blocks

The insurance office of the Montepio dos Empregados Municipais (1957) is to be built at an important crossroads in Rio de Janeiro. The 22-story building is planned with a steel frame. The treatment of the west façade, which is exposed to the glare of the sun, is particularly interesting; the variation in the sun-screens, combined with movable walls, imparts a quiet but intense life to the whole and forms a beautiful contrast to the glass front on the north side.

It is remarkable how often Reidy's plans betray an instinct for urban planning, a sense of harmony in difference. The most important of them so far, begun in 1947, is the housing development of Pedregulho, in Rio de Janeiro, planned for municipal clerks in a low-income bracket. As soon as I saw it at the 1951 Biennale, I realized that it would carry off the prize in its group.

The dominant note of Pedregulho is found in the serpentine line of block A on the height: seven stories, no elevator. Reidy merely exploits the site. A light concrete path leads from its highest point into the block, which is wonderfully brightened by the splendid open hall running through the entire length of the building. From this platform, two stories lead down into the lower apartments and the duplex apartments of the upper part. The serpentine line which gives pliability to the block — rigid fronts 200 yards long are regarded as inhuman — is a product of the configuration of the ground and the architect's eye. (With great courage, Alvar Aalto actually introduced it into the dormitory of the Massachusetts Institute of Technology in Cambridge, 1947—1949, and Le Corbusier proposed the same thing in somewhat terrifying dimensions in his design for the residential city in Algiers, 1931.) A special accent is given to the buttresses on which block A rests by the steep fall of the ground. They reappear in the free mezzanine floor, and elsewhere, too, this façade gives a strong feeling of security. Underneath the curving block lies the neighborhood center with gymnasium, swimming pool, playgrounds for children, market, small hospital, and straight residential blocks.

If we pass from building to building — from the delicate instrumentation of the interior, with a hint of blatancy in the exterior, by way of shaded ramps to the schoolhouse, then to the health center, on which special care is lavished in the ground plan and the architectural modeling of the details, and finally to the shopping center at the boundary of the site — there can be felt at every point an attractive freedom of the imagination, combined with careful consideration of the human factor. Whether it is derived from the southern sun or the Latin temperament, there is revealed throughout, as everywhere else in Brazilian architecture, a gift for structural effects, for the enlivenment of the flat wall surfaces of modern architecture — a highly important gift which no other country has developed to the same extent.

Pedregulho rises in the midst of chaos. Years were spent on its building. Why? The financing of nonspeculative building in Brazil is a slow process. But an important beginning has been made here: it has led to important results.

The plans for a pilots' training center in São Paulo (1947) contain, from the town-planning angle, a remarkable solution in the light but dense combination of the school zone, community center, and residential zone.

The plans for a new city center in Rio de Janeiro (1948) are interesting for their inclusion of historical buildings in the new plan and for the spatial connection of the low museum building with the multi-story administration offices. The connection between the high glass-fronted houses and the low blocks of flats, in the manner of Le Corbusier, is less convincing.

The plans for the housing development of Gávea in Rio de Janeiro, begun in 1952, are now completed. With its curving residential block, it is, in a way, a parallel to Pedregulho, though without the variety given by the parallel residential blocks.

A general survey of Affonso Eduardo Reidy's work shows that it is the town-planning elements which will assure him his specific standing in Brazilian architecture. A great country which has, up to now, had very little experience in town-planning — for reasons which cannot be gone into here — has set out to build a new capital, Brasilia. Situated at a high altitude in uninhabited territory, it is a gigantic project. For the first time in our age, a great city can be planned down to the smallest detail.

In the advanced seminary of the master's class at Harvard (Spring Term, 1958), we examined the planning of Brasilia in all its details and compared its scale with that of Washington, Paris, and Chandigarh. It turned out that the superblocks, which are a quarter of a mile long, are too small, and that there is an obvious danger of "beehive developments." The monumental artery proved to be three times as long as the distance between the Capitol and Washington's Monument in Washington, D. C., which itself almost outstrips human imagination.

There is a danger that the airplane-shaped plan, which is very attractive in two dimensions, may lose, when transferred into three, that inner tension of relationships which is the essence of every human settlement. The question therefore arises as to why the competition for such an important town plan on so huge a scale was not international and open to the most experienced town-planners. Why was Le Corbusier not invited, considering that he could have imparted to Brazil a second and ultimate impetus in town-planning? And why did Affonso Eduardo Reidy not enter? All this is quite beyond the conjecture of the present writer, but we must not abandon the hope that a few corrections in the human scale will be made in the boldest town-planning enterprise of our age. At this point, there is still time to correct a few errors. The beautifully stimulating buildings of Oscar Niemeyer need not be touched, but the exaggerated length of the monumental artery could be drastically reduced to come within the bounds of the human imagination, the superblocks could be assembled in bigger units, so that the wider developments which they involve could be grouped, and the entirely artificial traffic problems at the intersection of the two axes avoided.

S. Giedion

Hostel for Homeless Persons, Rio de Janeiro – 1931/32

with Gerson Pompeu Pinheiro
Structural engineer: Emílio Baumgart

The "Inn of Good Intentions" is a hostel for the homeless, for whom temporary accommodation has to be provided until they have found suitable work and housing.

The plan is developed around an inner courtyard of 5,400 sq. ft., which is freely spanned by the two middle first-floor dormitories. This arrangement permits a copious circulation of air, which is highly desirable because of the climate. The continuous series of windows on each of the long walls of the dormitories ensures that the rooms are well ventilated and lit.

The design was awarded first prize in an open competition.

Obdachlosenheim, Rio de Janeiro – 1931/32

Mit Gerson Pompeu Pinheiro
Statiker: Emílio Baumgart

Die »Herberge zum guten Willen« ist ein Heim für Obdachlose, denen vorübergehend Unterkunft gewährt werden soll, bis sie geeignete Arbeit und Wohnung gefunden haben.

Die Anlage entwickelt sich um einen 500 qm großen Innenhof, den die beiden mittleren Schlafsäle des Obergeschosses frei überspannen. Dadurch wird eine starke Luftzirkulation erreicht, die aus klimatischen Gründen sehr erwünscht ist. Die an beiden Längsseiten der Schlafsäle durchgehenden Fensterreihen gewährleisten eine gute Belüftung und Besonnung der Räume. Der Entwurf wurde in einem offenen Wettbewerb mit dem ersten Preis ausgezeichnet.

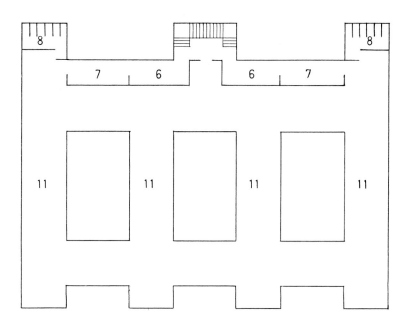

First-floor plan, scale 1:500 / Grundriß Obergeschoß

Ground-floor plan, scale 1:500 / Grundriß Erdgeschoß

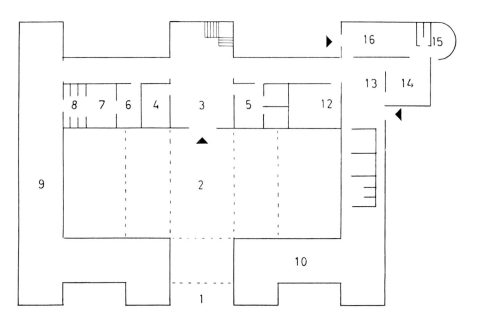

Captions to plans
Legende zu den Grundrissen
1 Entrance / Eingang
2 Inner courtyard / Innenhof
3 Reception / Empfang
4 Administration / Verwaltung
5 Medical examination
  Ärztliche Untersuchung
6 Cloakroom / Kleiderablage
7 Showers / Duschen
8 Lavatories / Toiletten
9 Women's dormitory / Frauenschlafsaal
10 Children's dormitory / Kinderschlafsaal
11 Men's dormitory / Männerschlafsaal
12 Storeroom / Lager
13 Canteen / Kantine
14 Kitchen / Küche
15 Food store / Vorratsraum
16 Disinfection room / Desinfektionsraum

View of the inner courtyard, freely spanned by dormitories.
Blick in den von Schlafsälen frei überspannten Innenhof.

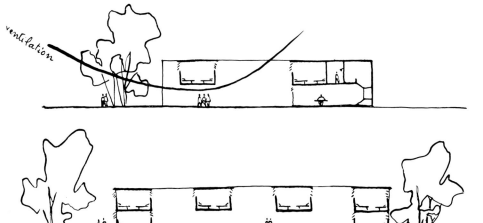

Air-circulation diagram / Schema der Luftzirkulation

Section through ground and first floor
Schnitt durch Erd- und Obergeschoß

Ministry of Education and Health,
Rio de Janeiro – 1937/43

The plans for this building, which is one of the most famous in Brazil, were the result of collaboration among the architects Lucio Costa, Carlos Leão, Jorge Moreira, Oscar Niemeyer, Affonso E. Reidy, Ernani Vasconcelos, Le Corbusier (as consultant), and the civil engineer Emílio Baumgart.

The fourteen-story block is at right angles to the main street, and is constructed on pillars which raise it 32 ft. 12 in. from ground level. In each of the ordinary stories, the three rows of supports allow any form of partitioning on either side of the central corridor, at each end of which are found the public and staff elevators, stairs, and lavatories. A lower wing, at right angles, contains a lecture room and exhibition hall. On the other side of the main block lies a smaller management annex, with entrance and elevators for staff. The raised second floor contains the Minister's rooms, which open on the roof garden over the exhibition hall.

As protection against the sun, the north façade is provided with a lattice of thin concrete ribs containing louvered screens of asbestos cement in metal frames.

Ministerium für Erziehung und Gesundheit,
Rio de Janeiro – 1937/43

Die Pläne für dieses wohl bekannteste Bauwerk Brasiliens entstanden in Zusammenarbeit zwischen den Architekten Lucio Costa, Carlos Leão, Jorge Moreira, Oscar Niemeyer, Affonso E. Reidy, Ernani Vasconcelos, Le Corbusier als Berater und dem Bauingenieur Emílio Baumgart.

Der 14-geschossige Block steht quer zur Hauptstraße und ist auf Pilotis konstruiert, die ihm einen Bodenabstand von 10 m geben. Die drei Stützenreihen ermöglichen in den Normalgeschossen jede Aufteilung auf beiden Seiten des Mittelganges, an dessen Enden sich die Publikums- und Personalaufzüge, Treppen und Toiletten befinden. Ein niedrigerer Querflügel enthält Vortragssaal und Ausstellungshalle. Auf der anderen Seite liegt ein kleiner Wirtschaftsanbau mit Eingang und Aufzügen für das Personal. Das überhöhte zweite Geschoß enthält die Räume des Ministers, die sich auf den Dachgarten über der Ausstellungshalle öffnen.

Die Nordfassade wurde zum Sonnenschutz mit einem Gitter dünner Betonrippen versehen, die verstellbare Blenden aus Asbestzement in Metallrahmen aufnehmen.

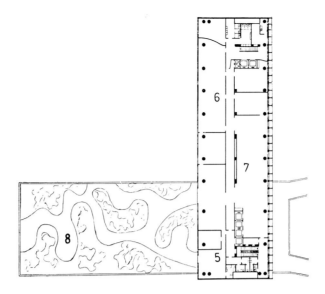

Raised first-floor plan, scale 1:1,000 / Grundriß erstes Obergeschoß

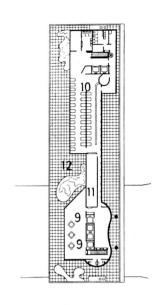

Roof floor plan, scale 1:1,000 / Grundriß Dachgeschoß

Ground-floor plan, scale 1:1,000 / Grundriß Erdgeschoß

Standard floor plan, scale 1:1,000 / Grundriß Normalgeschoß

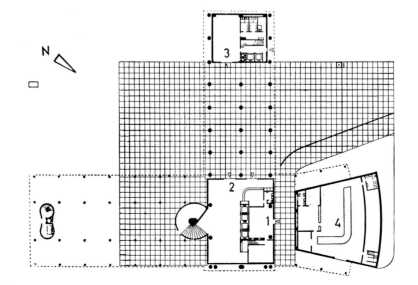

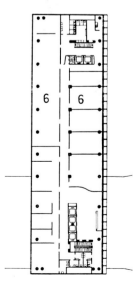

Captions to plans / Legende zu den Grundrissen
1 Minister's entrance / Eingang für den Minister
2 Public entrance / Publikumseingang
3 Staff entrance / Angestellteneingang
4 Cashier's office / Kasse
5 Minister's rooms / Räume des Ministers
6 Offices / Büroräume
7 Waiting room / Warteraum
8 Roof garden / Dachgarten
9 Minister's dining room / Speiseraum des Ministers
10 Staff dining hall / Speisesaal der Angestellten
11 Kitchen / Küche
12 Roof terrace / Dachterrasse

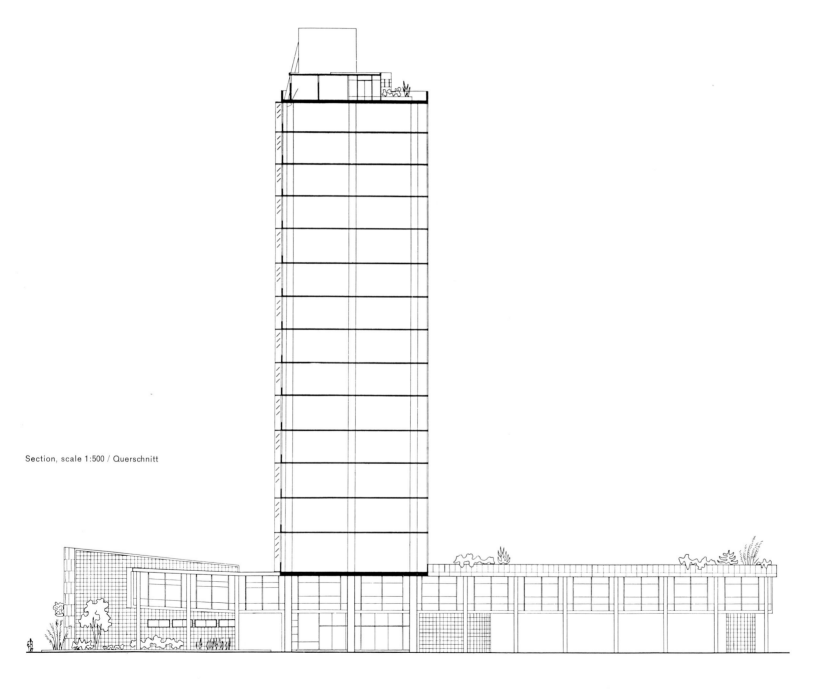

Section, scale 1:500 / Querschnitt

16

View of the south side. Contrast between the narrow slice of the main building and the lower wing at right angles to it.
Ansicht der Südseite. Kontrast zwischen der schmalen Scheibe des Hauptbaues und dem quergelagerten niedrigen Flügel.

The main structure on pillars 32 ft. 12 in. high. Open space and building mesh.
Der Haupttrakt auf 10 m hohen Pilotis. Freiraum und Baukörper durchdringen sich.

View of the south side. The cramped proportions of the site led to the extreme narrowness and height of the main building. Its roof story is decorated as a roof garden, as is that of the structure at right angles, and is accentuated by decorative constructions.
Ansicht der Südseite. Beengte Grundstücksverhältnisse führten zur schmalen, hohen Scheibenform des Hauptbaues. Sein Dachgeschoß ist wie das des Quertraktes als Dachgarten ausgestaltet und durch plastische Aufbauten akzentuiert.

Government Building for the Administration of the City Area, Rio de Janeiro – 1938

The Distrito Federal is an independently administered area which contains the city of Rio de Janeiro with its surroundings and suburbs. In 1938, the Palacio da Prefeitura was planned as the seat of this administration.

The complete structure covers an area of 690 x 430 ft. The eleven stories of the 525 ft.-long main building are supported by sixty-seven pillars. The south side (shadowed) is completely glazed; the north side contains a lattice of louvered screens, by which the working space is protected against the direct rays of the sun without any impairment of the uninterrupted view.

Ten stories serve to accommodate the offices, with subsidiary and utility rooms. A restaurant is on the eleventh story. Public and staff use independent entrances and circulation areas within the building.

The Prefect's offices are in the lower structure, from the upper story of which a corridor leads directly to the first upper story of the main building. On the mezzanine of the lower wing are located the inquiry office, halls with counters for public business, and an auditorium with foyer.

A garage is available for the cars of the higher officials; it is directly opposite the entrance to the Prefect's offices. There is an additional parking area in the immediate vicinity of the elevators of the main block.

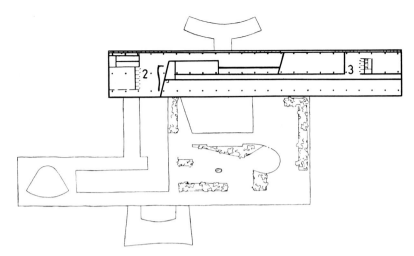

First-floor plan, scale 1:2,000 / Grundriß Obergeschoß

Mezzanine plan, scale 1:2,000 / Grundriß Hochparterre

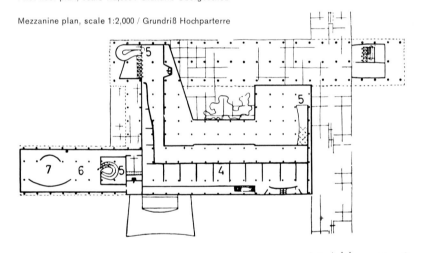

Ground-floor plan, scale 1:2,000 / Grundriß Erdgeschoß

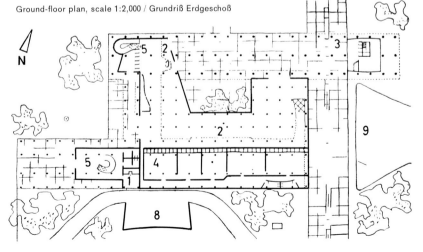

Captions to the plans
Legende zu den Grundrissen
1 Entrance to the Prefect's offices
  Eingang zu den Büroräumen des Präfekten
2 Public / Publikum
3 Staff / Angestellte
4 Service rooms / Diensträume
5 Ramp / Rampe
6 Foyer
7 Auditorium
8 Garage
9 Parking area / Parkplatz

Regierungsgebäude für die Verwaltung des Stadtbezirkes, Rio de Janeiro – 1938

Innerhalb des Staates Rio de Janeiro besteht der »Distrito Federal«, ein Bezirk, der die Stadt Rio de Janeiro mit Umgebung und Vororten einschließt und selbständig verwaltet wird. Im Jahre 1938 wurde der »Palacio da Prefeitura« als Sitz dieser Verwaltung geplant.

Die Gesamtanlage bedeckt eine Fläche von 210 x 130 m. Die 11 Geschosse des 160 m langen Hauptgebäudes werden von 67 Pilotis getragen. Die Südseite (Schattenseite) ist vollständig verglast, die Nordseite erhält ein Gitter aus Sonnenblenden, wodurch die Arbeitsplätze vor direkter Sonnenbestrahlung geschützt sind, ohne daß der freie Ausblick dadurch beeinträchtigt wird.

10 Geschosse dienen zur Unterbringung von Büros mit Zubehör- und Nebenräumen. Im 11. Geschoß befindet sich ein Restaurant. Publikum und Angestellte benützen voneinander unabhängige Eingänge und Verkehrswege innerhalb des Gebäudes.

Die Büros des Präfekten befinden sich in dem niedrigen Trakt, von dessen Obergeschoß eine direkte Verbindung zum ersten Obergeschoß des Hauptgebäudes führt. Im Hochparterre des niedrigen Flügels liegen Informationsdienst, Schalterräume und ein Auditorium mit Foyer.

Für die Wagen der höheren Beamten steht eine Garage zur Verfügung, die dem Eingang zu den Büros des Präfekten direkt gegenüber liegt. In unmittelbarer Nähe der Aufzüge des Hauptblocks befindet sich ein weiterer Parkplatz.

The north side, protected with louvered sun screens made from concrete units.
Die mit Sonnenblenden aus Betonelementen geschützte Nordseite.

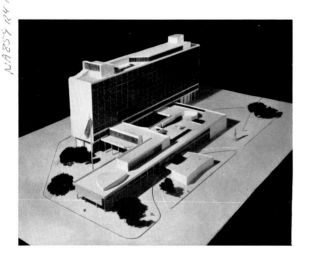

View of the model from the south. In the foreground, the lower structure with the Prefect's offices.
Ansicht des Modells von Süden. Im Vordergrund der niedrige Bautrakt mit den Büroräumen des Präfekten.

City Transport Service Offices with Workshops, Rio de Janeiro – 1939

The project consists of two parts: the workshops with an area of 97,000 sq. ft., and a five-story administration building that is 217 ft. long and 33 ft. wide.
The workshop part begins 66 ft. behind the building line and stretches over the entire remaining area, whose limits were determined by the irregular site available.
In order to obtain as uniform lighting of the working area as possible, as well as good ventilation of the workshops, double saw-tooth roofs were constructed, which are oriented north and south. Lattice-like screens to the north protect against direct sunlight. The whole workshop section is spanned by continuous cross-beams, from which the 39 ft.-wide hangar roofs are suspended.
Attached to the workshops are sanitary installations, dressing rooms, a kitchen, and a dining hall for 800 workers. The entrances for personnel and the transport drive-ins are separated.
The administration block stands on pillars, thus making almost the whole of the ground floor available for traffic flow and parking areas. There is a connection to the workshop section on the first upper story.

Direktion der Städtischen Verkehrsbetriebe mit Werkstätten, Rio de Janeiro – 1939

Das Projekt besteht aus zwei Teilen: den Werkstätten mit 9000 qm und einem 5-geschossigen Verwaltungsgebäude von 66 m Länge und 10 m Breite.
Der Werkstatteil beginnt 20 m hinter der Bauflucht und erstreckt sich über die ganze übrige Fläche, deren Begrenzung durch das zur Verfügung stehende unregelmäßige Grundstück bestimmt war.
Um eine möglichst gleichmäßige Belichtung der Arbeitsplätze und eine gute Durchlüftung der Werkstätten zu erzielen, wurden Doppelsheds konstruiert, die nach Süden und Norden orientiert sind. Gitterartige Blenden an den Nordseiten verhindern direkte Sonneneinstrahlung. Der gesamte Werkstatteil wird von durchlaufenden Querbalken überspannt, an denen mit 12 m Spannweite die Hallendächer aufgehängt sind.
Den Werkstätten angegliedert sind sanitäre Anlagen, Umkleideräume, eine Küche und ein Speisesaal für 800 Arbeiter. Die Personeneingänge und Einfahrten für Lastwagen liegen getrennt.
Der Verwaltungsblock steht auf Pilotis, wodurch fast das ganze Erdgeschoß für Verkehr und Parkplätze nutzbar gemacht wurde. Im ersten Obergeschoß besteht eine Verbindung zum Werkstatteil.

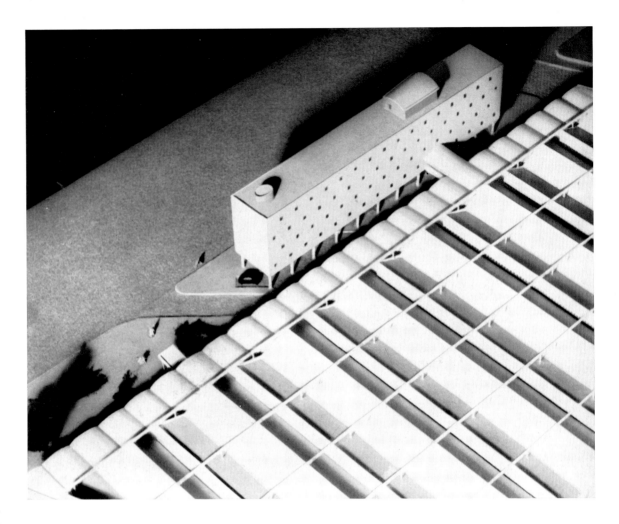

Workshop structure and rear of the administration building.
Werkstättentrakt und Rückseite des Verwaltungsgebäudes.

Section through workshop, scale 1:500
Schnitt durch den Werkstatteil

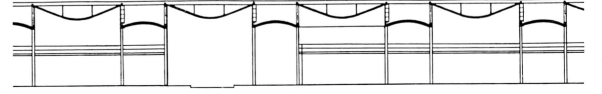

Street side of administration building with glazed façade.
Straßenseite des Verwaltungsgebäudes mit verglaster Fassade.

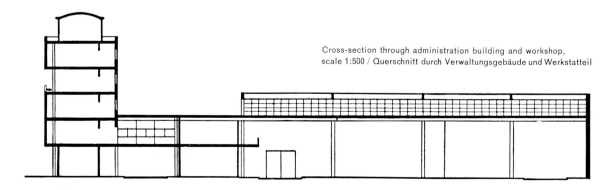

Cross-section through administration building and workshop,
scale 1:500 / Querschnitt durch Verwaltungsgebäude und Werkstatteil

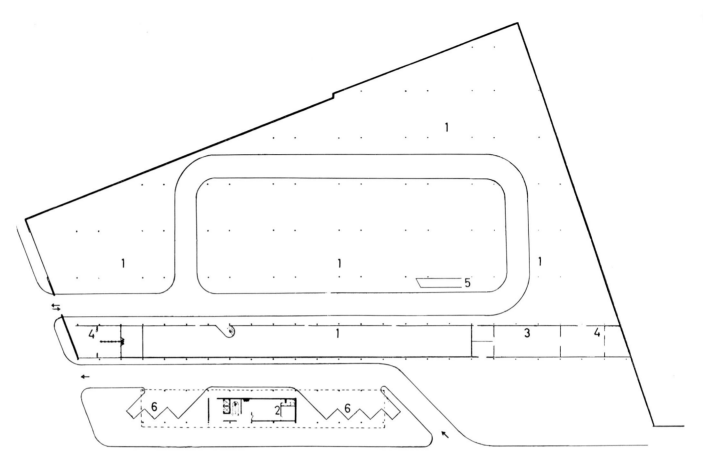

Ground-floor plan, scale 1:1,000 / Grundriß Erdgeschoß

Captions to the plans / Legende zu den Grundrissen
1 Workshops / Werkstätten
2 Offices / Büroräume
3 Dressing room / Umkleideraum
4 Lavatories / Toiletten
5 Ramp / Rampe
6 Parking areas / Parkplatz
7 Store / Lager
8 Canteen (office staff) / Kantine (Angestellte)
9 Kitchen / Küche
10 Canteen (workers) / Kantine (Arbeiter)
11 Management / Direktion
12 Veranda
13 Administration / Verwaltung
14 Lecture hall / Vortragssaal
15 Assembly room / Versammlungsraum

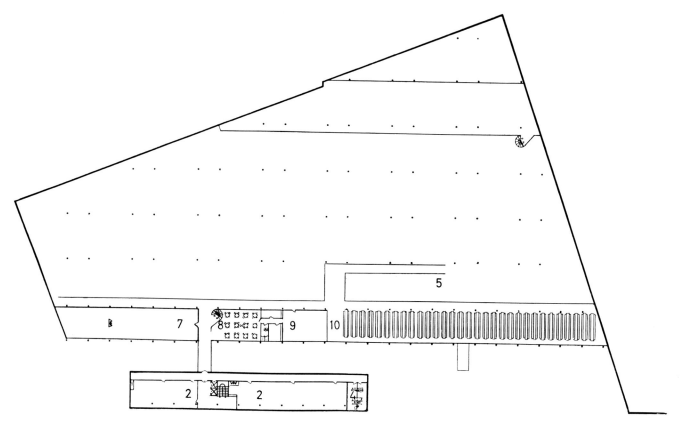

First upper-story plan, scale 1:1,000 / Grundriß 1. Obergeschoß

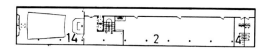

Second upper-story plan, scale 1:1,000 / Grundriß 2. Obergeschoß

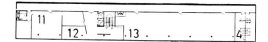

Third upper-story plan, scale 1:1,000 / Grundriß 3. Obergeschoß

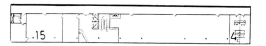

Fourth upper-story plan, scale 1:1,000 / Grundriß 4. Obergeschoß

Factory for Pharmaceutical and Cosmetic Products,
Rio de Janeiro – 1948

The design of this factory installation for the Sydney Ross Company had to take into account the triangular shape of a site on the road from Rio de Janeiro to Petropolis.

The roof of the main building is fanned upward on one side. This part is fully glazed at the front and contains three intermediate stories: two for offices and the uppermost for a restaurant with bar, day room, and terrace for office staff and managers. The works entrance leads over a long, gradually ascending ramp into the connecting story. Here are found clothes lockers for male and female workers, the entrance to the canteen, which is lodged in the lowest part, as well as stairs and elevators to the manufacturing shops. The upper story, intended for the main production, is lighted through saw-tooth roofs whose glazing is directed away from the sun.

Fabrik für pharmazeutisch-kosmetische Erzeugnisse,
Rio de Janeiro – 1948

Der Entwurf dieser Fabrikanlage für die Sydney Ross Co. hatte die dreieckige Form eines Grundstückes an der Straße Rio de Janeiro–Petropolis zu berücksichtigen.

Das Dach des Hauptgebäudes ist auf der einen Seite nach oben geschwungen. Dieser Teil ist auf der Stirnseite vollständig verglast und enthält drei Zwischengeschosse: zwei für Büroräume und das oberste für ein Restaurant mit Bar, Aufenthaltsraum und Terrasse für Büroangestellte und Direktoren. Der Werkeingang führt über eine lange, leicht ansteigende Rampe in das Verbindungsgeschoß. Hier befinden sich Garderobenschränke für Arbeiter und Arbeiterinnen, der Zugang zu der im niedrigsten Teil untergebrachten Kantine sowie Treppen und Aufzüge zu den Fabrikationshallen. Das für die Hauptproduktion vorgesehene Obergeschoß wird durch Sheds belichtet, deren Öffnungen zur sonnenfreien Seite gerichtet sind.

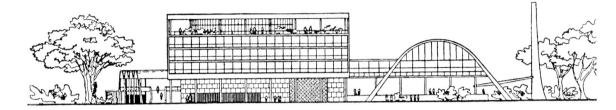

View from the southeast, scale 1:1,000 / Ansicht von Südosten

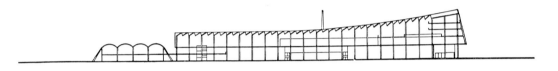

Section, scale 1:2,000 / Längsschnitt

Ground-floor plan, scale 1:2,000 / Grundriß Erdgeschoß

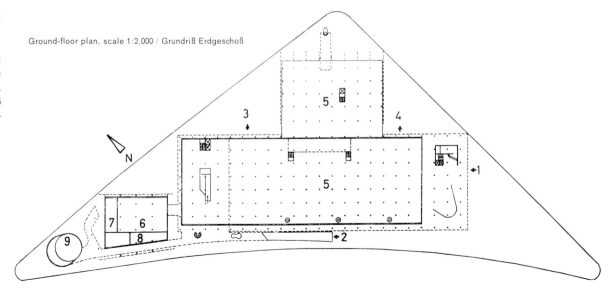

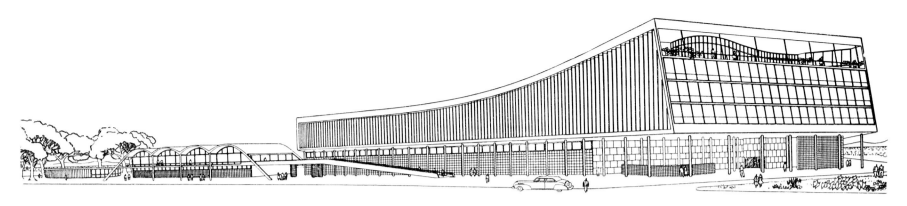

Perspective view from the south / Perspektive von Süden

Captions to the plans / Legende zu den Grundrissen
 1 Office entrance / Büroeingang
 2 Works entrance / Werkeingang
 3 Supply of materials / Materialzufuhr
 4 Delivery / Auslieferung
 5 Storage and packing rooms / Lager und Verpackung
 6 Garage
 7 Kitchen / Küche
 8 Medical department / Medizinische Abteilung
 9 Kindergarten
10 Canteen / Kantine
11 Ramp / Rampe
12 Control / Kontrolle
13 Cloakrooms / Garderoben
14 Lavatories / Toiletten
15 Production shed / Produktionshalle
16 Goods elevator and stairs / Materialaufzug und Treppe
17 Office elevator and stairs / Büroaufzug und Treppe
18 Entrance to lavatories / Toilettenzugang
19 Offices / Büroräume
20 Restaurant and bar / Restaurant und Bar
21 Terrace / Terrasse

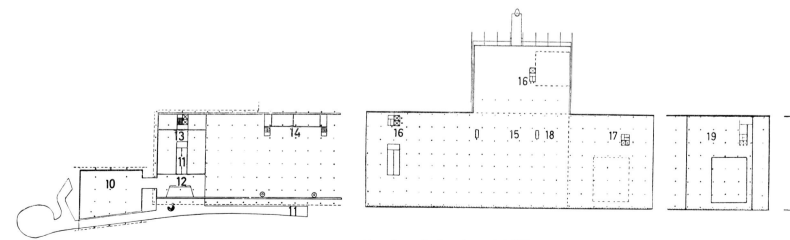

Intermediate-story plan, scale 1:2,000 / Grundriß Zwischengeschoß

Upper-floor and gallery plan, scale 1:2,000
Grundriß Obergeschoß und Galeriegeschosse

Pumping Installation, Rio de Janeiro – 1949

The pumping station has to raise sufficient pressure for the water supply of the Jardim Botanico and the Gávea district. A very beautiful site by the lagoon Rodrigo de Freitas was selected; this is an extensive lagoon lying between one of the beach areas and the city Botanical Gardens.

The sloping roof of the pump house extends down to ground level, allowing the greenery to grow over the whole roof.

The water tower has the form of an inverted, truncated, three-sided pyramid. Visitors can reach an intermediate story, from which the pumping installation can be inspected, by means of a ramp leading around the water tower.

Pumpanlage, Rio de Janeiro – 1949

Das Pumpwerk soll den für die Wasserversorgung der Stadtteile Jardim Botanico und Gávea notwendigen Druck aufbringen. Als Baugelände war ein sehr schönes Grundstück an der Lagune Rodrigo de Freitas vorgesehen, einer ausgedehnten Lagune, die zwischen einem Strandgebiet und dem Botanischen Garten der Stadt liegt.

Das schräge Pultdach des Pumpenhauses ist bis auf den Boden heruntergezogen und ermöglicht die Ausdehnung der Grünanlage über das ganze Dach hinweg. Der Wasserturm hat die Form eines umgekehrten dreiseitigen Pyramidenstumpfes. Über eine um den Wasserturm herumführende, begehbare Rampe können Besucher ein Zwischengeschoß erreichen, von dem aus die Pumpanlage besichtigt werden kann.

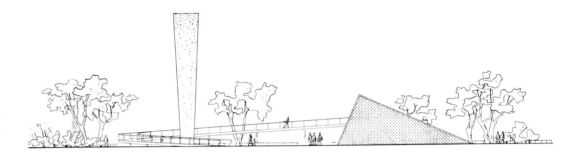

View, scale 1:500 / Ansicht

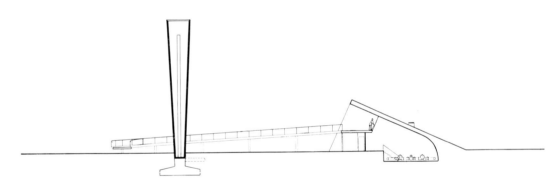

Section, scale 1:500 / Längsschnitt

Ground- and first-floor plan, scale 1:500 / Grundriß Erdgeschoß und Obergeschoß

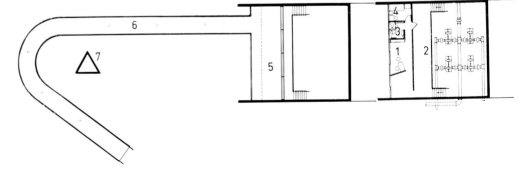

Captions to the plans / Legende zu den Grundrissen
1 Office / Büro
2 Pumping room / Pumpenraum
3 Showers and lavatories / Dusche und Toiletten
4 Superintendent's room / Raum des Aufsichtsbeamten
5 Terrace / Terrasse
6 Ramp / Rampe
7 Water tower / Wasserturm

Front view / Ansicht der Stirnseite

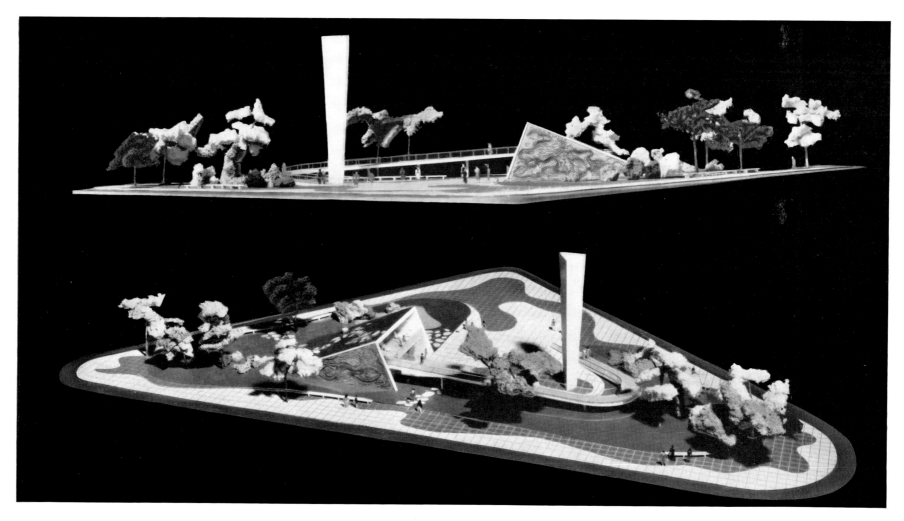

Office Building for the Central Administration of the Rio Grande do Sul Railway, Porto Alegre – 1944

with Jorge Machado Moreira

The design for this office building in reinforced concrete and glass arose out of a prize-winning competition project.

The twenty-two stories, supported by three rows of pillars, are built up on a hexagonal plan. Approximately 5 ft. outside the pillar structure continuous glass walls open all the upper stories to the south side, which gets no sun. On the opposite side, the necessary protection from the sun is obtained by means of vertically placed slats, which are fixed between the floors in front of the glass wall. There is only one internal row of pillars. The floor areas are simply partitioned, thus allowing a high degree of flexibility.

On the ground floor, the offices for direct public contact are located on either side of a vestibule. Separate entrances and elevators are provided for employees and officials. On the twentieth floor there is a restaurant seating 176, as well as a bar and kitchen. Over these, on the topmost floor, is located an auditorium, a common room, and a terrace with uninterrupted views in all directions over the city and river.

Bürogebäude für die Zentralverwaltung der Rio-Grande-do-Sul-Eisenbahn, Porto Alegre – 1944

Mit Jorge Machado Moreira

Der Entwurf für dieses Bürogebäude aus Stahlbeton und Glas ist aus einem preisgekrönten Wettbewerbsprojekt hervorgegangen.

Die 22 Geschosse, getragen von drei Säulenreihen, bauen sich auf hexagonalem Grundriß auf. Etwa 1,5 m außerhalb der Säulenstruktur öffnen durchgehende Glaswände sämtliche Obergeschosse dem sonnenfreien Südlicht. Auf der gegenüberliegenden Seite wird der nötige Sonnenschutz durch vertikal gestellte Lamellen erreicht, die vor der Glaswand zwischen den Geschoßdecken angebracht sind. Es gibt nur eine einzige innere Stützenreihe. Die Geschoßflächen sind einfach unterteilt und gewährleisten einen hohen Grad an Flexibilität.

Im Erdgeschoß liegen auf beiden Seiten einer Vorhalle die Büroräume für den direkten Publikumsverkehr. Für Angestellte und Beamte sind getrennte Eingänge und Aufzüge vorgesehen. Im 20. Obergeschoß befindet sich ein Restaurant mit 176 Plätzen sowie eine Bar und Küche. Darüber liegen im obersten Geschoß ein Auditorium, ein Gesellschaftsraum und eine Terrasse.

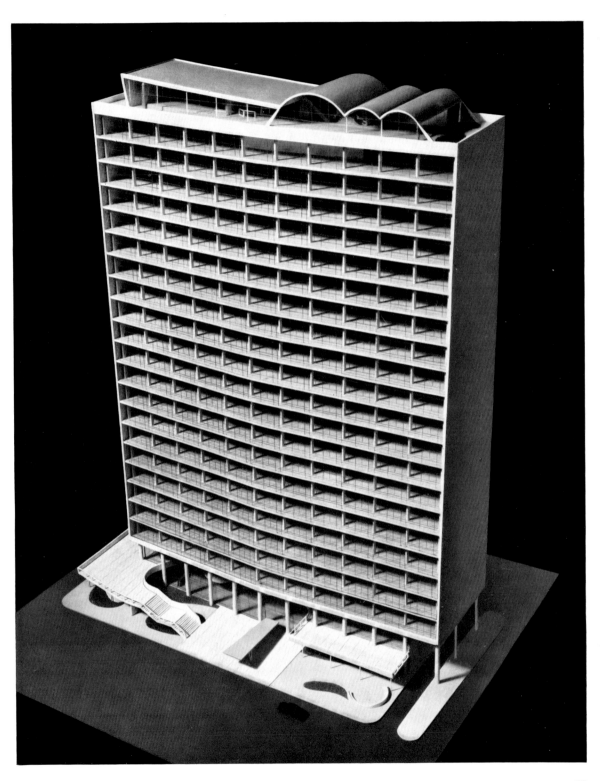

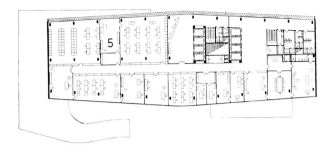

Standard-floor (first to nineteenth stories) plan, scale 1:1,000
Grundriß eines Normalgeschosses (1.—19. Obergeschoß)

◁ View of the south side / Ansicht der Südseite

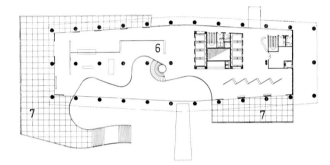

Mezzanine floor plan, scale 1:1,000 / Grundriß Hochparterre

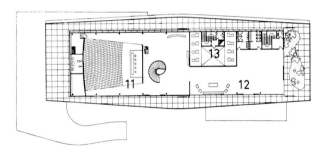

Twenty-first-floor plan, scale 1:1,000 / Grundriß 21. Obergeschoß

Cross-section, scale 1:1,000 / Querschnitt

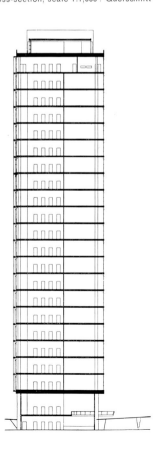

Ground-floor plan, scale 1:1,000 / Grundriß Erdgeschoß

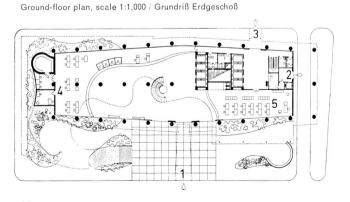

Twentieth-floor plan, scale 1:1,000 / Grundriß 20. Obergeschoß

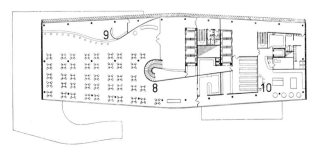

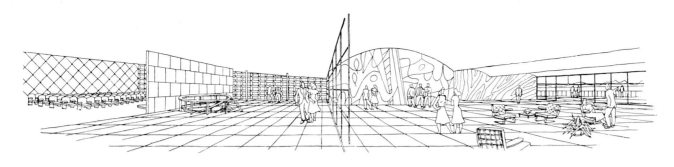

Twenty-first story, with auditorium and common room
21. Obergeschoß mit Auditorium und Gesellschaftsraum

Twentieth story, with restaurant and bar
20. Obergeschoß mit Restaurant und Bar

Ground floor, with entrance hall / Erdgeschoß mit Eingangshalle

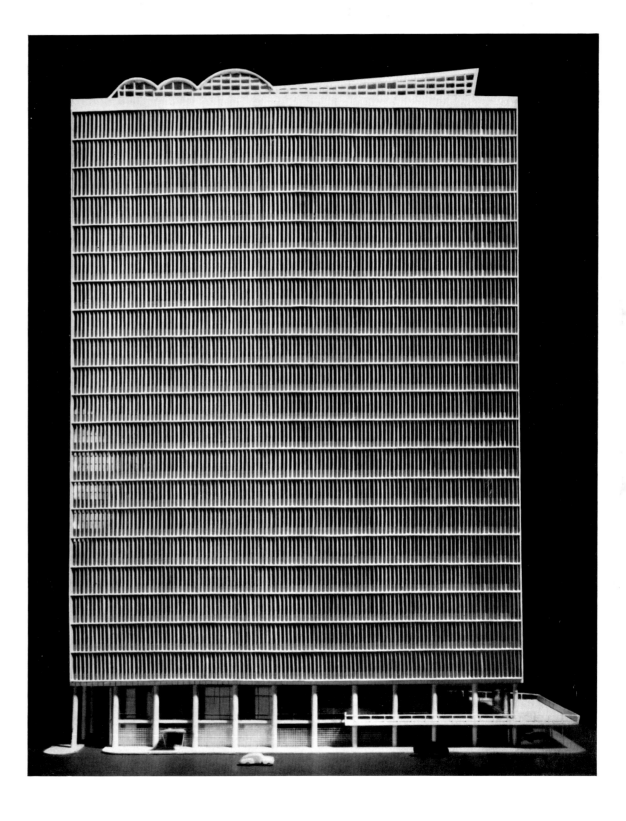

North side clad with sun-screen slats.
Die mit Sonnenschutzelementen verkleidete Nordseite.

33

Project for an Insurance Building (Montepio dos Empregados Municipais), Rio de Janeiro – 1957

Structural engineer: Paulo Fragoso

The town planning of Rio de Janeiro provides for the reconstruction of one part of the city center, particularly along the Avenida Presidente Vargas. This building is to be erected where this wide street crosses the planned north-south thoroughfare, and is intended to accommodate an insurance office for municipal employees.

The twenty-two stories are to be erected as a steel-frame building, a mode of construction that has seldom been used before in Brazil, although it has the advantages of smaller cross-sections for beams and pillars and greater speed of erection when compared to ferroconcrete. The position, shape, and size of the pillars on the ground floor must be in accordance with the building regulations as published for the reconstruction of the Avenida Presidente Vargas.

The south side is suitable for the arrangement of office space, since it remains in shadow for almost the whole year. This façade will be completely glazed. The west façade, strongly exposed to the sun, is equipped with a special sun-screen system. This consists of a fixed reinforced concrete lattice and adjustable aluminum blinds. The reinforced concrete lattice, which has broad and narrow openings, will be fixed at a certain distance in front of the façade, allowing air to circulate directly in front of the window areas and thus improving the ventilation of the rooms. The broad openings are equipped with venetian blinds made of adjustable aluminum slats. This system ensures that the view outside is unimpaired when the sun is not shining. When the blinds are fully closed, the narrow units of the grid, which always remain open, provide sufficient ventilation. The contrast between the irregularity of the movable elements and the fixed and immovable part gives to the façade plasticity and rhythm.

Part of the west facade, with the sun-screen system made of reinforced concrete lattices and adjustable aluminum slats.
Ausschnitt aus der Westfassade mit dem Sonnenschutzsystem aus Stahlbetongittern und verstellbaren Aluminiumlamellen.

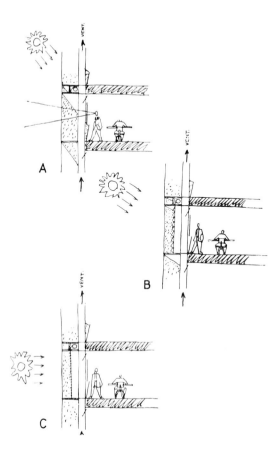

The effect of the sun-screen units at different positions of the sun:
A Reinforced concrete grid sufficient, providing open view
B Aluminum blinds half open
C Aluminum blinds closed

Die Wirkung der Sonnenschutzelemente bei verschiedenem Sonnenstand:
A Stahlbetongitter ausreichend, freie Sicht nach außen
B Aluminiumblenden halb geöffnet
C Aluminiumblenden geschlossen

Projekt für ein Versicherungsgebäude (Montepio dos Empregados Municipais), Rio de Janeiro – 1957

Statiker: Paulo Fragoso

Die Stadtplanung von Rio de Janeiro sieht für einen Teil des Zentrums, besonders entlang der Avenida Presidente Vargas, eine Neubebauung vor. An der Kreuzung dieser großen Straße mit der geplanten Nord-Süd-Verbindung soll dieses Gebäude errichtet werden, das ein Versicherungsinstitut für die städtischen Angestellten aufnehmen wird.

Die 22 Geschosse werden in Stahlkonstruktion aufgeführt, die in Brasilien bisher nur selten zur Anwendung kam, gegenüber einer Stahlbetonkonstruktion jedoch die Vorteile geringerer Balken- und Stützenquerschnitte und eines schnelleren Aufbaues aufweist. Die Position, Form und Größe der Säulen im Erdgeschoß müssen den Bauvorschriften entsprechen, wie sie für die Bebauung der Avenida Presidente Vargas herausgegeben wurden.

Für die Anordnung von Büroräumen ist die Südseite günstig, weil sie fast das ganze Jahr über im Schatten bleibt. Diese Fassade wird vollständig verglast. Die stark der Sonne ausgesetzte Westfassade ist mit einem besonderen Sonnenschutzsystem versehen. Es besteht aus einem feststehenden Stahlbetongitter und verstellbaren Aluminiumblenden. Das Stahlbetongitter, das breite und schmale Öffnungen aufweist, wird in einem bestimmten Abstand vor der Fassade angebracht, um unmittelbar vor den Fensterflächen eine Luftzirkulation zu ermöglichen und die Belüftung der Räume zu fördern. Die breiten Öffnungen sind mit Jalousien aus verstellbaren Aluminiumlamellen versehen. Durch dieses System wird die Sicht nach außen während der sonnenfreien Stunden nicht beeinträchtigt. Bei vollständig geschlossenen Jalousien sorgen die immer offen bleibenden schmalen Einheiten des Rasters für ausreichende Ventilation. Durch die Unregelmäßigkeit der beweglichen Elemente innerhalb des straffen Systems der festen Teile wirkt die Fassade in ihrer plastischen Gliederung sehr lebendig.

General view of the model with the fully glazed south side.
Gesamtansicht des Modells mit der voll verglasten Südseite.

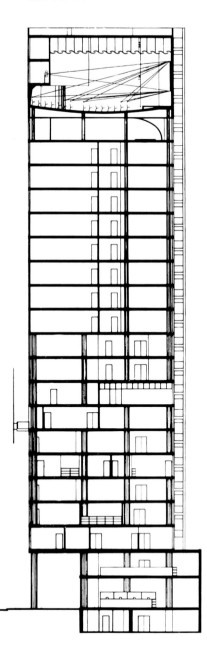

Cross-section / Schnitt

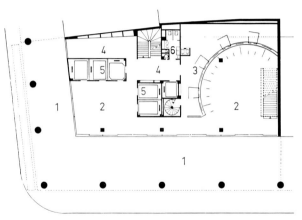

Ground-floor plan, scale 1:500 / Grundriß Erdgeschoß

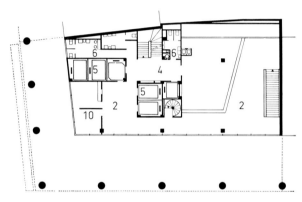

Standard-floor plan, scale 1:500 / Grundriß Normalgeschoß

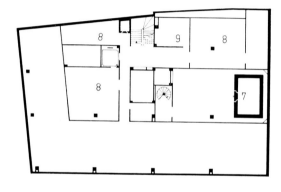

Plan of basement, scale 1:500 / Grundriß Kellergeschoß

Mezzanine floor plan, scale 1:500 / Grundriß Hochparterre

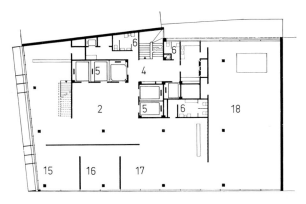

Eighteenth-floor plan, scale 1:500 / Grundriß 18. Obergeschoß

Twenty-first-floor plan, scale 1:500 / Grundriß 21. Obergeschoß

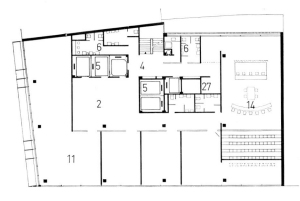

Sixteenth-floor plan, scale 1:500 / Grundriß 16. Obergeschoß

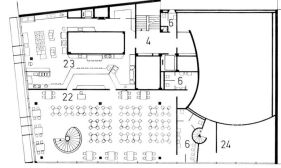

Twentieth-floor plan, scale 1:500 / Grundriß 20. Obergeschoß

Sixth-floor plan, scale 1:500 / Grundriß 6. Obergeschoß

Nineteenth-floor plan, scale 1:500 / Grundriß 19. Obergeschoß

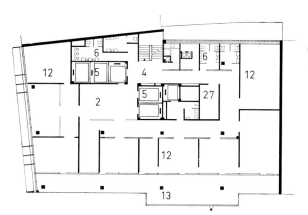

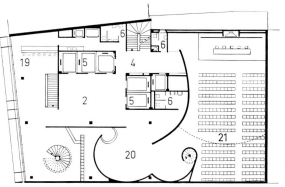

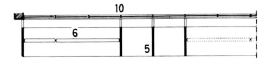

Horizontal section C-D through the sun-screen system of the west façade
Horizontalschnitt C-D durch das Sonnenschutzsystem der Westfassade

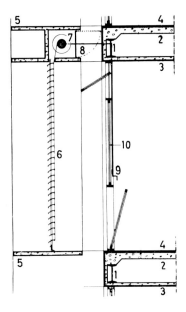

Vertical section A-B through the sun-screen system of the west façade
Vertikalschnitt A-B durch das Sonnenschutzsystem der Westfassade

Diagram of the west façade (part)
Schema der Westfassade (Ausschnitt)

Captions to details of façade / Legende zu den Fassadendetails
1 Steel girder / Stahlträger
2 Reinforced concrete ceiling / Stahlbetondecke
3 Ceiling / Plafond
4 Floor / Fußboden
5 Fixed sun-screen unit made of 2³/₈ in.-thick reinforced concrete
  Feste Sonnenschutzelemente aus Stahlbeton in 6 cm Stärke
6 Venetian blinds with adjustable aluminum slats
  Jalousien mit verstellbaren Aluminiumlamellen
7 Roller blind / Rouleau
8 Roller-blind case / Rouleaukasten
9 Operating mechanism / Bedienungsvorrichtung
10 Window / Fenster

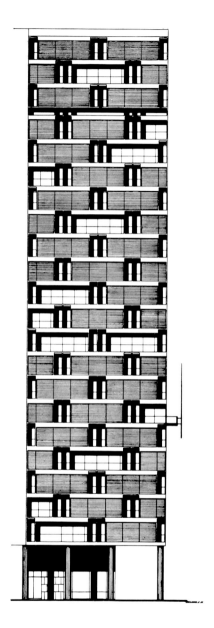

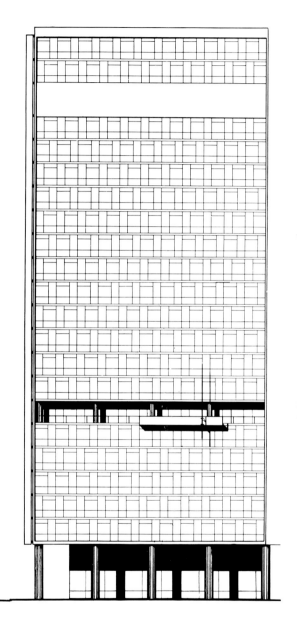

View of west side, scale 1:500 / Ansicht der Westseite

View of south side, scale 1:500 / Ansicht der Südseite

Community Theater, Rio de Janeiro – 1950/51

This small theater was commissioned by the city administration and built in Marechal Hermes, an industrial quarter of Rio de Janeiro. The building is surrounded by a garden, designed by Roberto Burle-Marx. The intention was to provide here a small cultural center to stimulate the residents' interest in the theater, music, and dance, as well as to arrange conferences and smaller exhibitions.

In front of the entrance, a screen roof protects the billboards and box office. The foyer is reached through a wide revolving glass door; so also are the cloakrooms and the spiral staircases, which lead to a mezzanine floor, on which the sanitary installations are located.

The auditorium holds 300 people; it is insulated with cork slabs. The decor of the stage, which is approximately 100 ft. wide, is movable—either around the floor on rollers or up to the ceiling on rails. Artists' dressing rooms and lavatories are behind the stage.

Volkstheater, Rio de Janeiro – 1950/51

Dieses kleine Theater wurde von der Stadtverwaltung in Auftrag gegeben und in Marechal Hermes, einem Industrieviertel von Rio de Janeiro erbaut. Das Gebäude ist von einem Garten umgeben, den Roberto Burle-Marx gestaltet hat. Es war beabsichtigt, hier ein kleines kulturelles Zentrum zu schaffen und das Interesse der Bevölkerung für Theater, Musik und Tanz zu wecken sowie Zusammenkünfte und kleinere Ausstellungen zu veranstalten.

Vor dem Eingang schützt ein Schirmdach Anschlagtafeln und Kasse. Durch eine breite Drehtür aus Glas gelangt man in das Foyer, zu den Garderoben und den Wendeltreppen, die in ein Zwischengeschoß führen, in dem die sanitären Einrichtungen untergebracht sind.

Der Zuschauerraum faßt 300 Personen und ist mit Korkplatten isoliert. Die Dekorationen der etwa 30 m breiten Bühne sind verschiebbar, sie können entweder auf Rollen am Boden oder auf Schienen an der Decke bewegt werden. Hinter der Bühne befinden sich Künstlergarderoben und Toiletten.

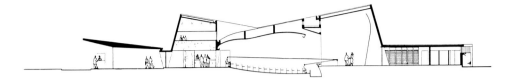

Section, scale 1:500 / Längsschnitt

Ground plan, scale 1:500 / Grundriß

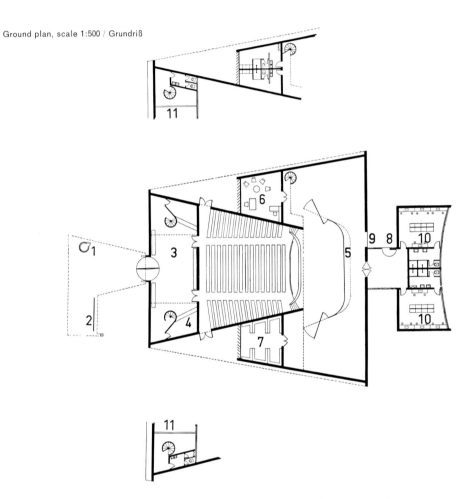

Captions to ground plan / Legende zum Grundriß
1 Box office / Kartenverkauf
2 Billboards / Anschlagtafeln
3 Foyer
4 Cloakroom / Garderobe
5 Cyclorama / Rundprospekt
6 Administration / Verwaltung
7 Costumes / Kostüme
8 Stage door / Eingang für Schauspieler
9 Staff entrance / Personaleingang
10 Players' dressing rooms / Schauspielergarderoben
11 Mezzanine, with lavatories / Zwischengeschosse mit Toiletten

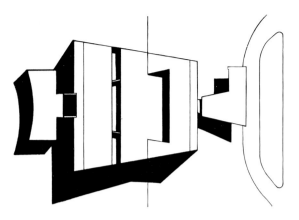

View from above and site plan / Aufsicht und Lageplan
General view, with front roof / Gesamtansicht mit Vordach

Side view of stage and auditorium. The walls of the wings are covered
with ceramic tiles, designed by Paulo Werneck.
Seitenansicht von Bühnen- und Zuschauerhaus. Die Wände des Bühnen-
flügels sind mit Keramikplatten verkleidet, deren Entwurf von Paulo
Werneck stammt.

Interior view of the auditorium with 300 seats. Curtain designed by Roberto Burle-Marx, executed by Lili Corrêa de Araujo.
Innenansicht des Zuschauerraumes mit 300 Sitzplätzen. Bühnenvorhang nach einem Entwurf von Roberto Burle-Marx, ausgeführt von Lili Corrêa de Araujo.

The foyer, with one of the side galleries. Left, the entrance to the auditorium.
Das Foyer mit einer Seitengalerie. Links der Zugang zum Zuschauerraum.

Student Theater, Rio de Janeiro – 1955

This theater is to be built in Campo Grande, a suburb of Rio de Janeiro, for a student organization concerned with the popularization of the theater in the outlying districts of the city. It is not intended as a commercial theater, but as a meeting point for all interested in theater—a place where amateur groups will have the opportunity to organize themselves and to rehearse and perform plays.

The stage is 46 ft. wide, 30 ft. deep, and 38 ft. high (up to the gridiron). The maximum proscenium opening is 25 x 15 ft. The auditorium contains 242 seats, which are arranged in ascending rows. Auditorium and stage can be combined by planking in the area, and the theater is thus converted into a ballroom.

In one part of the basement are artists' dressing rooms and rooms for stage equipment, and in the other part, which is separate, there is a canteen. Near the building is a swimming pool, measuring 39 x 20 ft., with dressing rooms.

Studententheater, Rio de Janeiro – 1955

Dieses Theater soll in Campo Grande, einem Vorort von Rio de Janeiro, für eine Studentenorganisation gebaut werden, die sich mit der Popularisierung des Theaters in den ländlichen Gegenden des Stadtbezirkes beschäftigt. Es ist nicht als kommerzielles Theater gedacht, sondern als Treffpunkt für alle am Theater Interessierten, und soll Laiengruppen die Möglichkeit zum Aufbau, Proben und Spielen geben.

Die Bühne ist 14 m breit, 9 m tief und bis zum Schnürboden 11,70 m hoch. Die maximale Bühnenöffnung beträgt 7,50 x 4,50 m. Der Zuschauerraum enthält 242 Plätze, die in ansteigenden Reihen angeordnet sind. Durch Überdeckung können Zuschauerraum und Bühne zu einer großen Fläche verbunden und das Theater in einen Ballsaal verwandelt werden.

In dem einen Teil des Untergeschosses liegen Künstlergarderoben und Zubehörräume für die Bühne, im anderen Teil, unabhängig davon, eine Kantine. Neben dem Gebäude befindet sich ein Schwimmbecken von 12,50 x 6,00 m mit Umkleidekabinen.

Model. View from the south / Modell. Ansicht von Süden

44

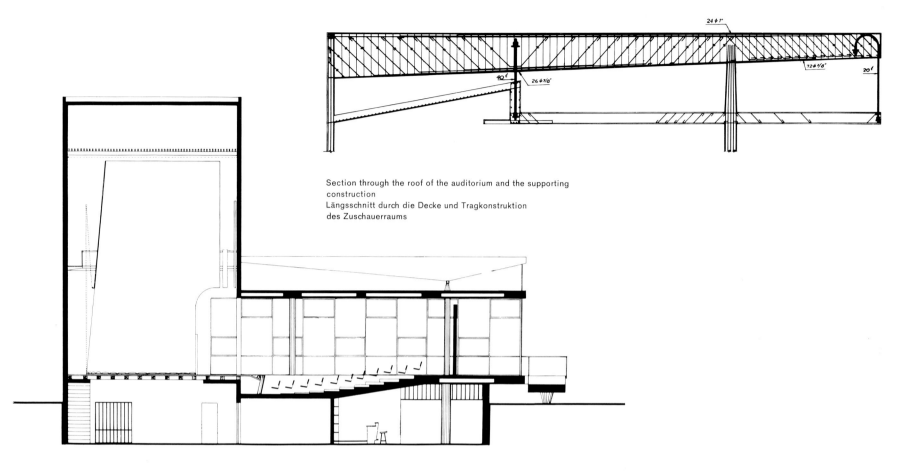

Section through the roof of the auditorium and the supporting
construction
Längsschnitt durch die Decke und Tragkonstruktion
des Zuschauerraums

Section, scale 1:200 / Längsschnitt

Interior perspective view of the foyer and auditorium
Innenperspektive von Foyer und Zuschauerraum

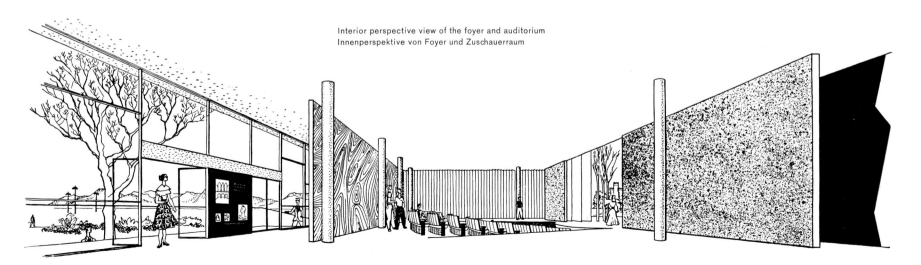

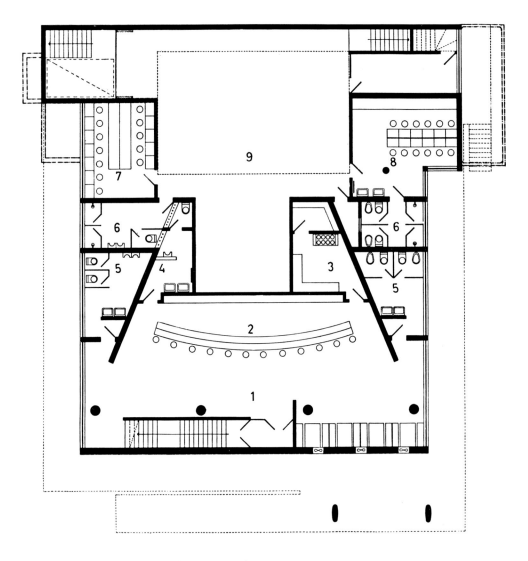

Captions to the plans / Legende zu den Grundrissen
1 Canteen / Kantine
2 Bar
3 Kitchen / Küche
4 Lavatory (personnel) / Toilette (Personal)
5 Lavatory (public) / Toilette (Publikum)
6 Lavatories and showers / Toiletten und Duschen
7 Dressing room (actors) / Garderobe (Schauspieler)
8 Dressing room (actresses) / Garderobe (Schauspielerinnen)
9 Stage equipment / Bühnenzubehör
10 Ramp / Rampe
11 Foyer
12 Cloakroom / Garderobe
13 Stalls / Parkett
14 Stage / Bühne
15 Secretariat / Sekretariat
16 Administration / Verwaltung
17 Swimming pool / Schwimmbad
18 Dressing rooms / Umkleideräume

Basement plan, scale 1:200 / Grundriß Untergeschoß

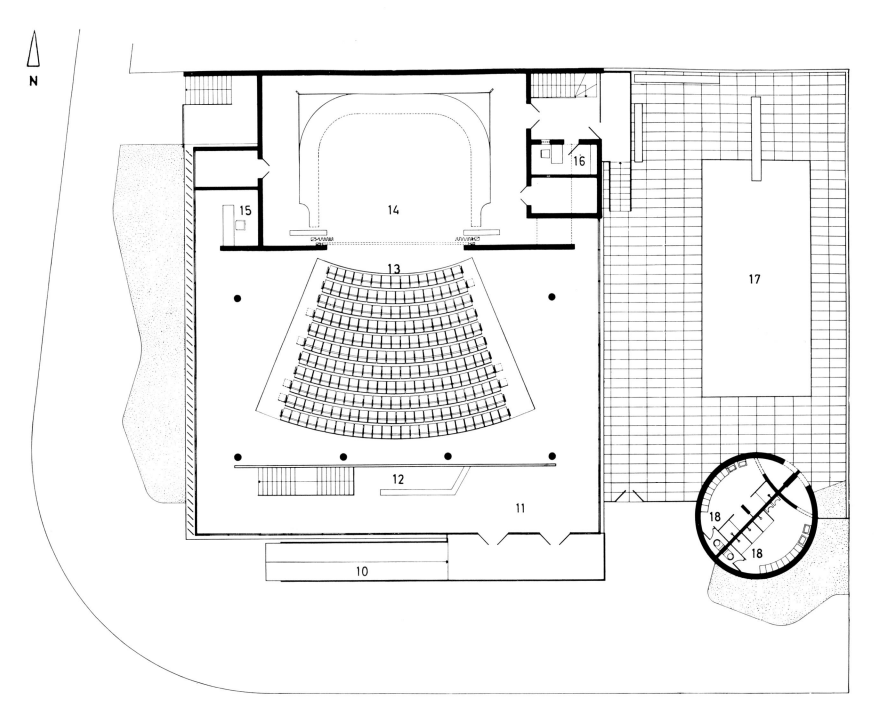

N

15

14

16

13

17

12

11

10

18

18

Upper-floor plan, scale 1:200 / Grundriß oberes Geschoß

Model. View from southeast. Foreground, swimming pool and
dressing rooms.
Modell. Ansicht von Südosten. Vorne Schwimmbecken
und Umkleideräume.

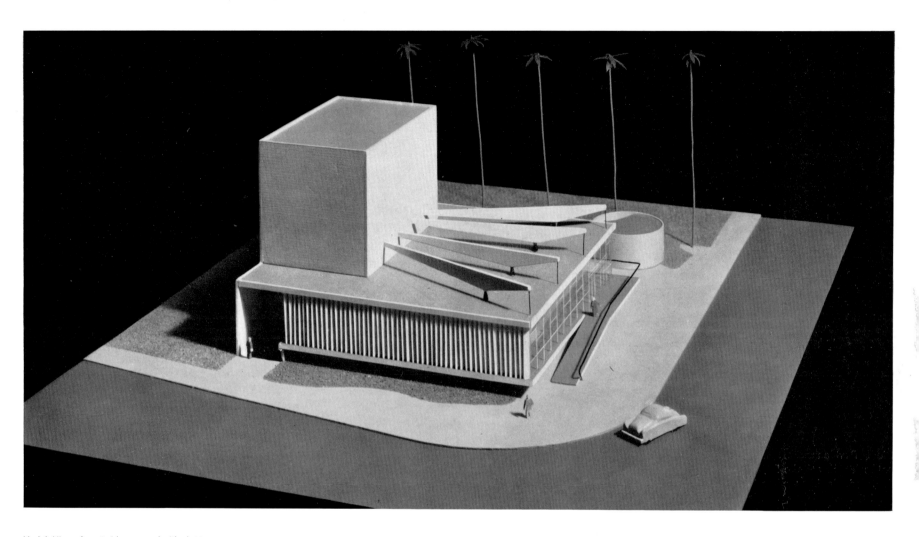

Model. View of west side, covered with slat-type sun screen.
Modell. Ansicht der Westseite, die mit lamellenförmigen
Sonnenblenden verkleidet ist.

Pavilion on the Lagoon Rodrigo de Freitas, Rio de Janeiro – 1957

The design for this pavilion was commissioned by the municipal government. It is intended to accommodate the offices of the special technical service entrusted with the protection and care of the lagoon, as well as those of the Society of Friends of the Lagoon. The purpose of the society is to open up to tourism the area around the lagoon, and to promote its development from the town-planning point of view in collaboration with the municipal government.

The pavilion consists essentially of assembled wooden elements. A notable feature is the separation of the roof structure from the rooms below. The building stands on piles which rise 4 ft. from the ground. The latticework of the roof is supported on twelve pillars. Since the roof is separated from the building proper, the heat generated on the roof by the sun cannot be transmitted to the rooms below. The air circulating under the roof and under the floor ensures pleasant climatic conditions. The sides of the pavilion receiving most sunlight are provided with adjustable venetian blinds of aluminum which are fitted outside so that the sun's rays do not shine directly on the glazed surfaces of the façade.

Pavillon an der Lagune Rodrigo de Freitas, Rio de Janeiro – 1957

Dieser Pavillon wurde im Auftrag der Stadtverwaltung entworfen. Er soll die Büros des mit dem Schutz und der Pflege der Lagune beschäftigten technischen Spezialdienstes und die »Gesellschaft der Freunde der Lagune« aufnehmen. Diese Gesellschaft versucht, das Lagunengebiet städtebaulich und touristisch zu erschließen.

Der Pavillon setzt sich im wesentlichen aus Holz-Montagebauteilen zusammen. Bemerkenswert ist die Trennung von Dach- und Raumkonstruktion. Das Gebäude steht auf Pfählen, die 1,20 m aus dem Boden ragen. Die Fachwerkkonstruktion des Daches wird von 12 Stützen getragen. Durch die Ablösung des Daches vom eigentlichen Baukörper kann sich die auf dem Dach durch Sonnenstrahlung entstehende Wärme nicht auf die Räume übertragen. Sowohl unter dem Dach als auch unter dem Fußboden entsteht eine Luftzirkulation, die entsprechend günstige klimatische Bedingungen schafft. Die am meisten der Sonne ausgesetzten Seiten des Pavillons werden mit verstellbaren Aluminiumlamellen ausgestattet, die außen angebracht sind, so daß die Sonnenstrahlen nicht auf die verglasten Oberflächen der Fassade treffen.

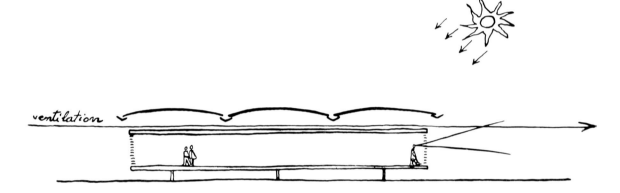

Ventilation system / Belüftungsschema

View of model from the north / Modellansicht von Norden

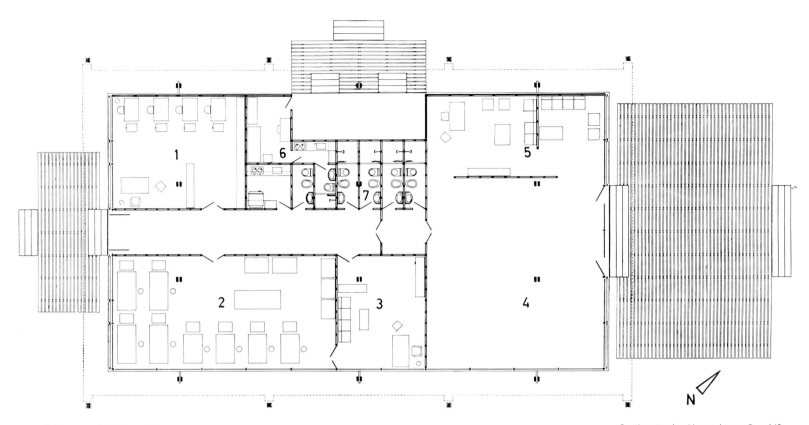

Ground plan, scale 1:200 / Grundriß

View of model from the east / Modellansicht von Osten

N

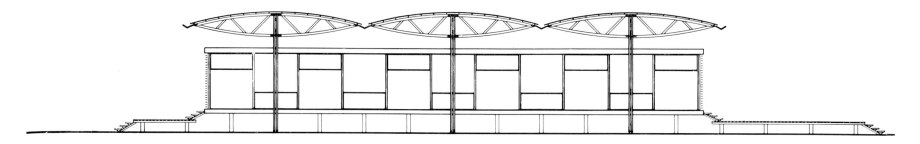

View from the southeast, scale 1:200 / Südostansicht

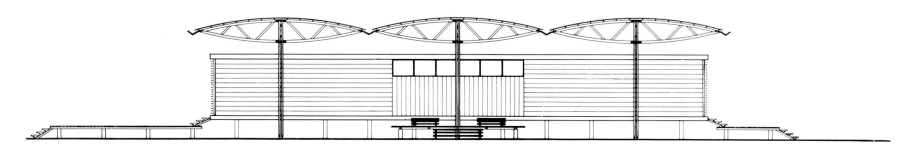

View from the northwest, scale 1:200 / Nordwestansicht

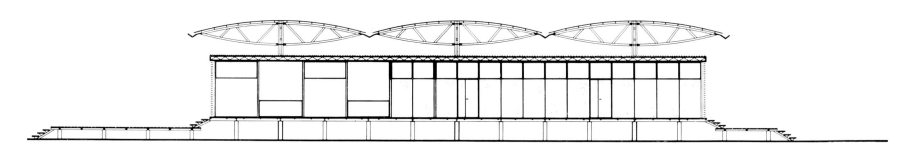

Longitudinal section, scale 1:200 / Längsschnitt

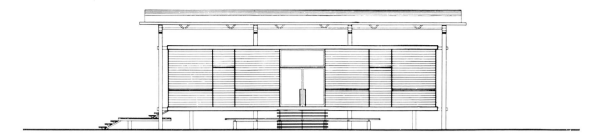

View from the southwest, scale 1:200 / Südwestansicht

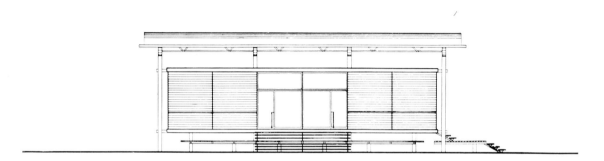

View from the northeast, scale 1:200 / Nordostansicht

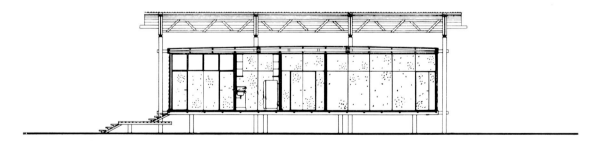

Cross-section, scale 1:200 / Querschnitt

53

Museum of Visual Arts, São Paulo – 1952

The plan to build this museum as a three-sided prism originated in the attempt to combine a clean-cut form with the best possible exploitation of the irregular site.
The axis of the equilateral triangle is at right angles to the Avenida Paulista, one of the main thoroughfares of São Paulo. Access to the museum is from this side. On the ground floor, a hall with freely curved external walls accommodates the secretariat, ticket office, cloakrooms, and a stall for the sale of publications. This floor is almost entirely open and merges with a platform affording uninterrupted views of the town. As a result of the marked difference in levels, the story below this platform is very high; it has been designed as a theater seating 1,000. Storerooms, repair shops, and the department handling the arrival and dispatching of goods are also accommodated here.
An escalator capable of carrying 6,000 persons per hour leads from the entrance hall into the stories where the exhibitions are held. Access is also gained by means of a ramp shaped like a horseshoe. As an economy measure, this ramp is also used as the only means of exit.
The top floor is intended to house a library, an auditorium, and a bar or restaurant. A water tank, the machine room for the elevators, and a small apartment for the caretaker are accommodated on the roof. Sections have been cut out of the ceilings of the various stories, and these afford unexpected views of the floors below, as well as an opportunity to set up tall pieces of sculpture. The exhibition areas are completely free and permit works of art to be displayed in any arrangement. Movable elements are provided for hanging pictures, and these can also be arranged as required.
Good natural lighting is ensured by the glazing on all sides and by additional light from above the ramp. Sunscreens are necessary on two of the three façades of the building: the north side has been provided with a ceramic lattice, and the south side with movable sunblinds.
A freight elevator is provided for transporting paintings and works of sculpture, and there is a small passenger elevator for the museum staff.

Museum für bildende Künste, São Paulo – 1952

Der Plan, dieses Museum als dreiseitiges Prisma zu bauen, entstand aus dem Bestreben, eine klare und reine Form mit der besten Ausnutzung des unregelmäßigen Grundstücks zu vereinen.
Die Achse des gleichschenkligen Dreiecks steht im rechten Winkel zur Avenida Paulista, einer der großen Hauptstraßen São Paulos. Von hier erfolgt der Zugang zum Museum. Im Erdgeschoß befinden sich in einer Halle mit frei gekurvten Außenwänden das Sekretariat, der Kartenverkauf, die Garderoben und ein Verkaufsstand für Publikationen. Dieses Geschoß ist fast völlig offen und geht in eine Plattform über, die einen ungestörten Ausblick über die Stadt vermittelt. Durch die starken Niveauunterschiede ergibt sich unter dieser Plattform ein sehr hohes Geschoß, das für ein Theater mit 1000 Plätzen vorgesehen ist. Außerdem befinden sich hier Lagerräume, Reparaturwerkstätten und die Ein- und Auslieferungsabteilung.
Von der Eingangshalle aus führt eine Rolltreppe mit einer Transportkapazität von 6000 Personen pro Stunde in die Ausstellungsgeschosse. Eine weitere Verbindung bildet eine hufeisenförmig gebogene Rampe. Um erhöhte Kosten zu vermeiden, erfolgt der Abgang nur über diese Rampe.
Das oberste Geschoß soll eine Bibliothek, ein Auditorium und eine Bar oder ein Restaurant aufnehmen. Auf dem Dach befinden sich der Maschinenraum für die Aufzüge, ein Wasserspeicher und eine kleine Wohnung für den Museumsdiener.
In den Geschoßdecken befinden sich mehrere Ausschnitte, die eine Reihe von überraschenden Perspektiven in die darunterliegenden Geschosse und gleichzeitig die Möglichkeit zum Aufstellen hoher Skulpturen bieten. Die Ausstellungsflächen sind vollkommen frei und erlauben eine beliebige Anordnung der Kunstwerke. Für die Ausstellung von Bildern sind bewegliche Platten vorgesehen, die ebenfalls je nach Bedarf angeordnet werden können.
Durch allseitige Verglasung und durch zusätzlichen Lichteinfall oberhalb der Rampe ist eine gute natürliche Belichtung gesichert. Zwei der drei Fassaden des Baukörpers müssen Sonnenschutzvorrichtungen erhalten: die Nordseite ist mit einem Keramikgitter versehen, die Südseite mit beweglichen Sonnenblenden.
Für den Transport von Plastiken und Bildern ist ein Lastenaufzug, für den internen Dienst des Museums ein kleinerer Personenaufzug vorgesehen.

Captions to the plans / Legende zu den Grundrissen
1 Entrance / Eingang
2 Cloakroom / Garderobe
3 Escalator / Rolltreppe
4 Ramp / Rampe
5 Elevators / Aufzüge
6 Lavatories / Toiletten
7 Theater
8 Hall / Halle
9 Storerooms and workshops / Lager und Werkstätten
10 Exhibitions / Ausstellungen
11 Perforation / Deckenausschnitt
12 Picture storage / Bildermagazin
13 Bar
14 Library / Bibliothek
15 Auditorium
16 Caretaker's apartment / Wohnung des Museumsdieners
17 Machine room / Maschinenraum

Site plan / Lageplan

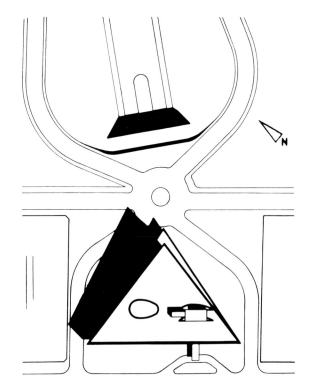

54

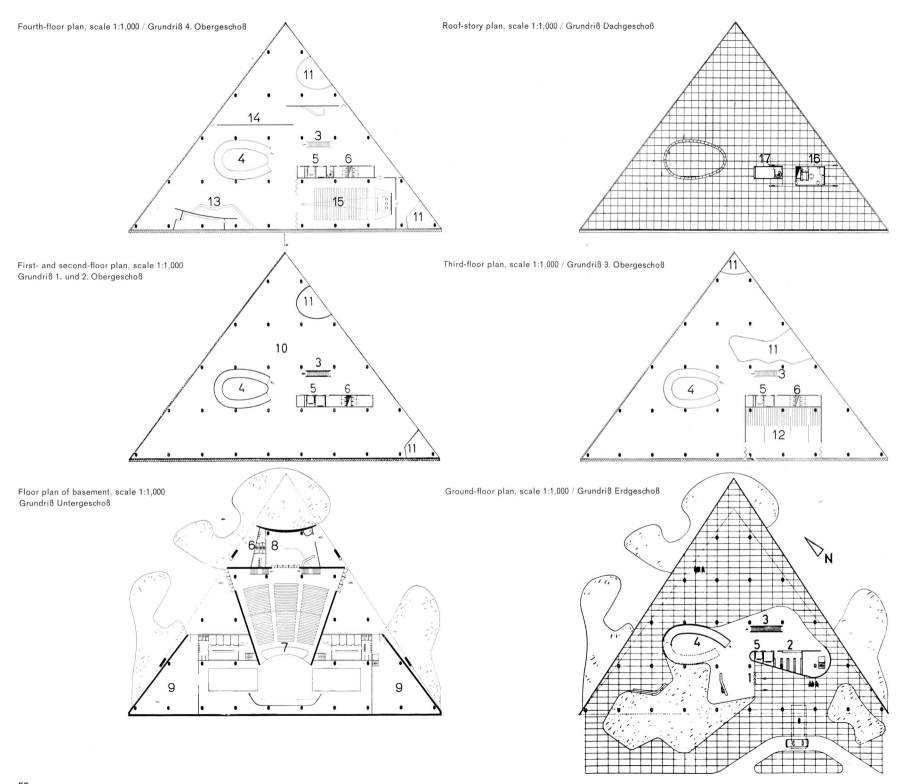

Fourth-floor plan, scale 1:1,000 / Grundriß 4. Obergeschoß

Roof-story plan, scale 1:1,000 / Grundriß Dachgeschoß

First- and second-floor plan, scale 1:1,000
Grundriß 1. und 2. Obergeschoß

Third-floor plan, scale 1:1,000 / Grundriß 3. Obergeschoß

Floor plan of basement, scale 1:1,000
Grundriß Untergeschoß

Ground-floor plan, scale 1:1,000 / Grundriß Erdgeschoß

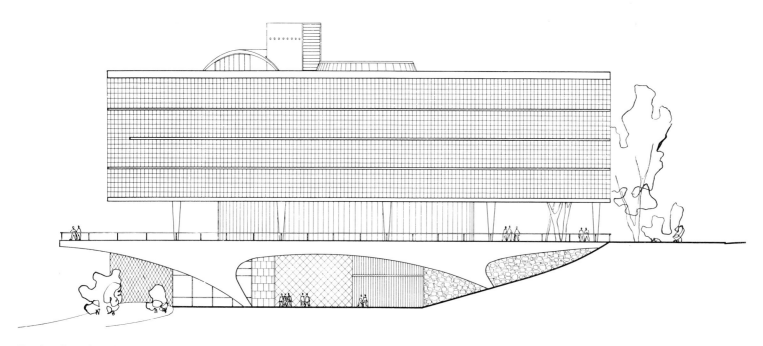

View from the north, scale 1:500 / Ansicht von Norden

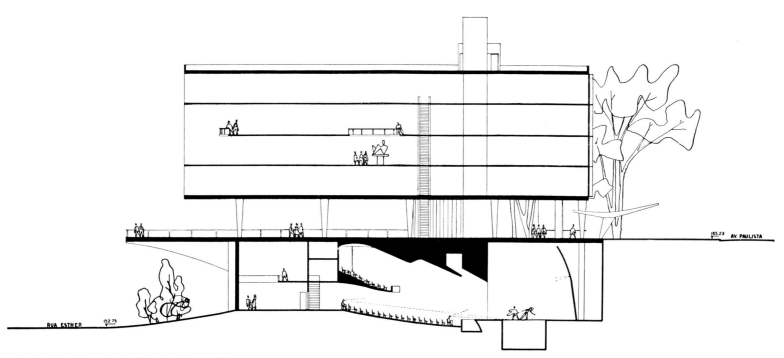

Section along the southwest-northeast axis, scale 1:500
Schnitt in der Südwest/Nordost-Achse

56

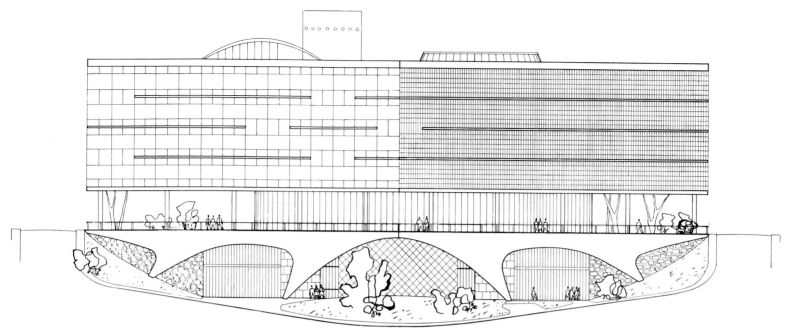

View from the northeast, scale 1:500 / Ansicht von Nordosten

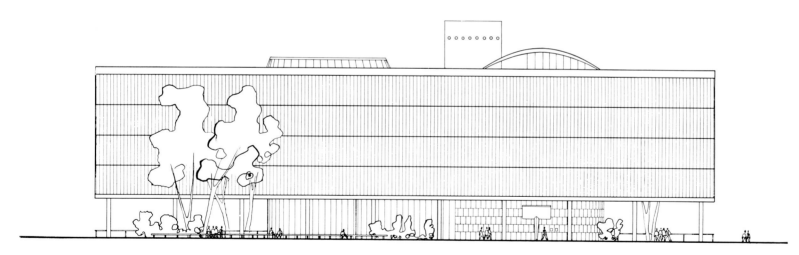

View from the southwest, scale 1:500 / Ansicht von Südwesten

Experimental School in Asunción, Paraguay – 1953
Structural engineer: Sydney Santos

This school is a gift to Paraguay from the Brazilian Government. It is an experimental teacher's training college forming part of Paraguay's new university city of Yta-Pyta-Punta. The building occupies two of the standard lots available for the development of the university city. The elevated position affords an extensive view as far as distant Chaco.

The site, which is slightly inclined in an east-west direction, is rectangular in shape, the north side being occupied for almost its entire length by the teaching building. The building is thus located away from the main street and combines freedom from disturbance with the best views.

In winter, the north façade receives the full light of the sun. For this reason, the bearing-reinforced concrete frames were made to project sufficiently to form screening ribs and also to accommodate canopy-like sun blinds in front of the classroom windows.

The ground floor of this block is almost entirely open, thus creating a shady place between the pillars where students can gather between classes. A long ramp leads to a corridor from which access is gained to the classrooms. The corridors of the upper stories pass over and under the passages connecting the classroom block with the other parts of the school: auditorium, gymnasium, and swimming pool. These are on the side nearest the road, so that access to buildings used for communal activities may be gained without disturbing classes. The arrangement of the auditorium and swimming pool was governed partly by a desire to take advantage of the natural slope of the site in order to cut down the cost of ground leveling.

Versuchsschule in Asunción, Paraguay – 1953
Statiker: Sydney Santos

Diese Schule ist ein Geschenk der brasilianischen Regierung an Paraguay. Es handelt sich um eine experimentelle Lehrerbildungsanstalt, die ein Teil von Paraguays neuer Universitätsstadt Yta-Pyta-Punta ist. Die Anlage nimmt zwei von den Standardgrundstücken ein, die für den Ausbau der Universitätsstadt zur Verfügung stehen. Die erhöhte Lage gewährt eine weite Sicht.

Das Gelände, das leicht in Ost-West-Richtung fällt, hat die Form eines Rechtecks, dessen Nordseite fast in seiner ganzen Länge von dem Unterrichtsgebäude eingenommen wird. Auf diese Weise liegt der Bau von der Hauptstraße abgewandt und vereinigt Ruhe mit bester Aussichtslage.

Im Winter erhält die Nordfassade volle Sonnenbestrahlung. Deshalb wurden die tragenden Stahlbetonrahmen so weit nach außen gezogen, daß sie schützende Rippen bilden und außerdem über den Klassenfenstern markisenartige Sonnenblenden aufnehmen können.

Das Erdgeschoß dieses Blocks ist fast vollständig offen. So entsteht zwischen den Pilotis ein schattiger Pausenhof. Eine lange Rampe führt hinauf zu einem Korridor, von dem aus die Klassenräume zugänglich sind. Die Verkehrswege der Obergeschosse verlaufen über und unter den Übergängen, die den Klassenblock mit den übrigen Teilen der Gesamtanlage verbinden: Auditorium, Turnhalle und Schwimmbad. Diese liegen zur Straße hin, so daß der Zugang zu den gemeinschaftlich benutzten Einrichtungen ohne eine Störung des Unterrichtsbetriebs möglich ist. Bei der Anordnung von Auditorium und Schwimmbad war die Überlegung mitbestimmend, bei den Erdbewegungen das natürliche Gefälle des Grundstücks so ökonomisch wie möglich auszunutzen.

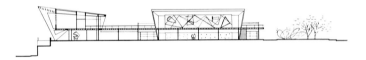

Section through the terrace, scale 1:1,000 / Schnitt durch die Terrasse

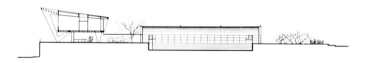

Axial section through the gymnasium, scale 1:1,000
Achsialschnitt durch die Turnhalle

Section through the swimming pool, scale 1:1,000
Schnitt durch das Schwimmbecken

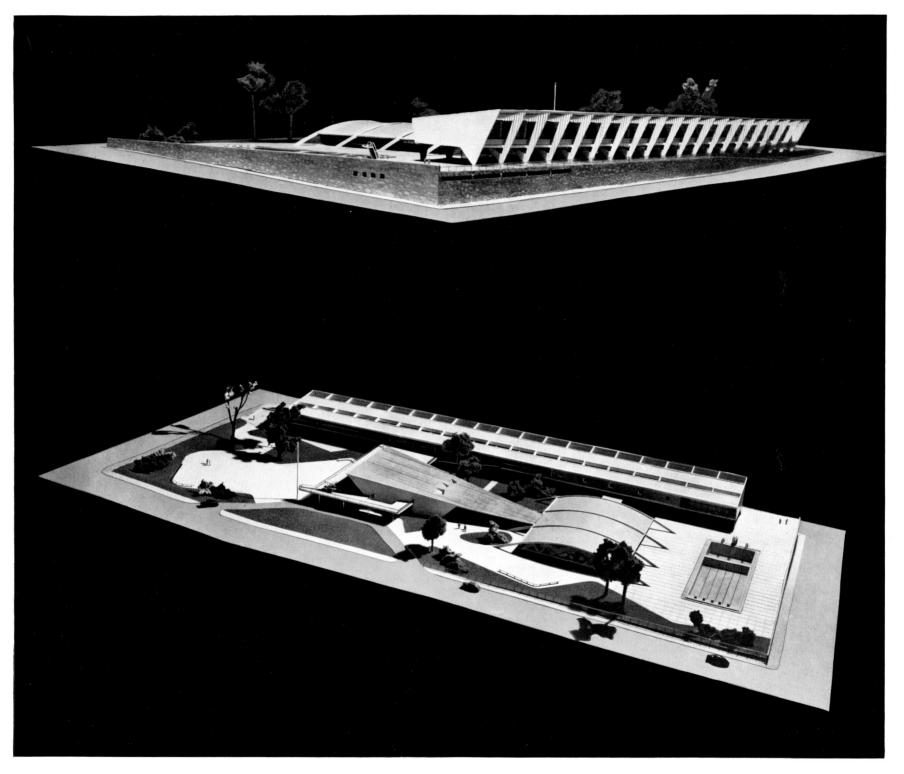

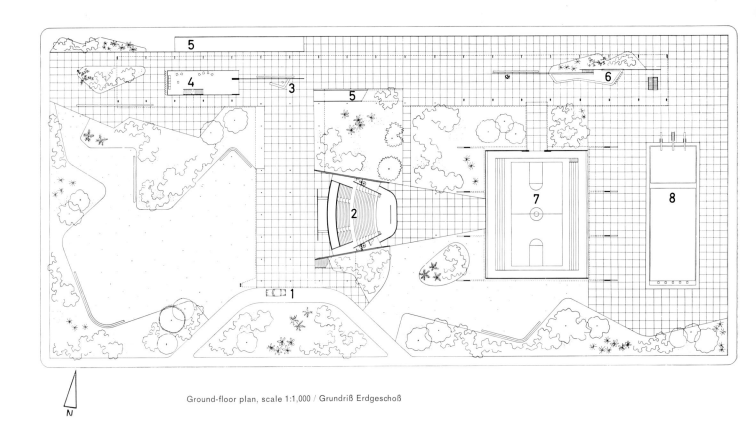

Ground-floor plan, scale 1:1,000 / Grundriß Erdgeschoß

N

Upper-floor plan, scale 1:1,000 / Grundriß Obergeschoß

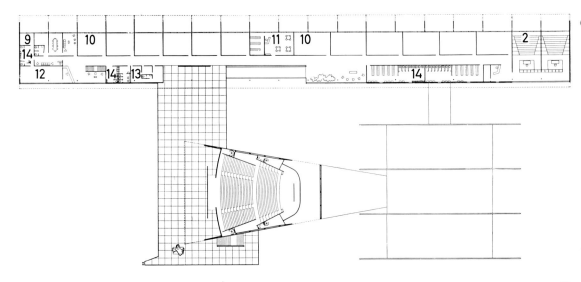

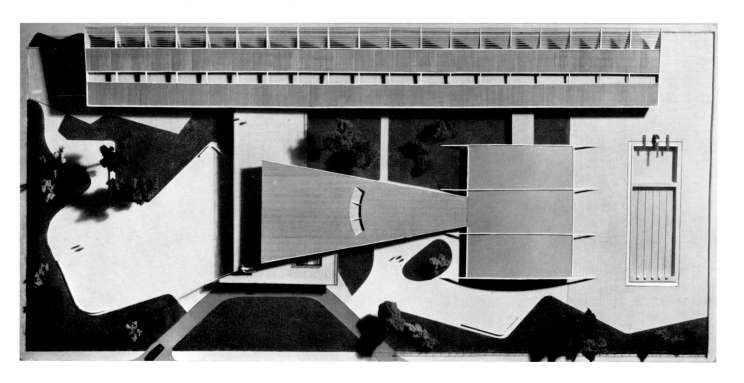

Site plan, scale 1:1,000 / Lageplan

Floor plan of basement, scale 1:1,000 / Grundriß Kellergeschoß

Captions to plans / Legende zu den Grundrissen
1 Main entrance / Haupteingang
2 Auditorium
3 Inquiries / Anmeldung
4 Day room / Aufenthaltsraum
5 Ramp / Rampe
6 Canteen / Kantine
7 Gymnasium / Turnhalle
8 Swimming pool / Schwimmbecken
9 Director / Direktor
10 Classrooms / Klassenräume
11 Library / Bibliothek
12 Secretariat / Sekretariat
13 Doctor and dentist / Arzt und Zahnarzt
14 Lavatories / Toiletten
15 Showers / Duschen
16 Dressing rooms / Umkleideräume

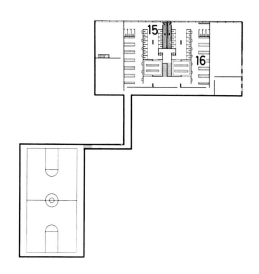

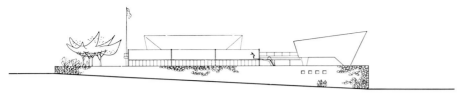

View from the east, scale 1:1,000 / Ostansicht

View from the north, scale 1:1,000 / Nordansicht

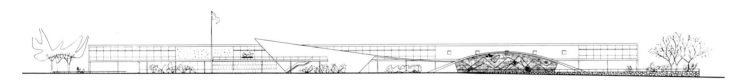

View from the south, scale 1:1,000 / Südansicht

Axial section through the auditorium, scale 1:1,000
Achsialschnitt durch das Auditorium

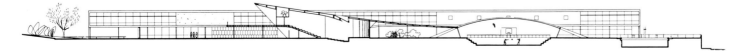

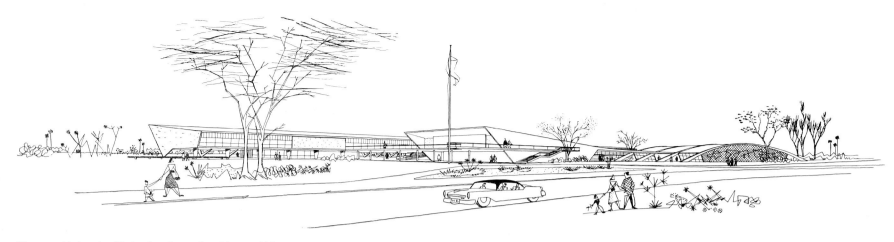

Classroom block and auditorium from the southwest (street side).
Klassenblock und Auditorium von Südwesten (Straßenseite).

North side of the classroom block. Sun-screen elements set in the reinforced concrete.
Nordseite des Klassenblocks. In die Stahlbetonrahmen eingespannte Sonnenschutzelemente.

Access ramp on the courtyard side of the classroom block.
Zugangsrampe auf der Hofseite des Klassenblocks.

North side of the classroom block.
Nordseite des Klassenblocks.

In winter, the north façade receives the full light of the sun. For this reason, the bearing-reinforced concrete frames were made to project sufficiently to form screening ribs and also to accommodate canopy-like sun blinds in front of the classroom windows.

Im Winter erhält die Nordfassade volle Sonnenbestrahlung. Deshalb wurden die tragenden Stahlbetonrahmen so weit nach außen gezogen, daß sie schützende Rippen bilden und außerdem über den Klassenfenstern markisenartige Sonnenblenden aufnehmen können.

Museum of Modern Art, Rio de Janeiro
commenced 1954

Structural engineers: Serviços de engentraria Emílio Baumgart and Escritorio tecnico da Companhia Construtora Nacional S.A.

The scope of this museum is not limited merely to art exhibitions and lectures. The intention was rather to develop an arts center comprising the museum itself, a school with lecture and work rooms, and a theater seating 1,000 persons for plays, concerts, ballets, film showings, and conferences.

The details given below are taken from an essay by the architect. He first quotes the words with which the museum prefaced the provisional plans for its new building:

"The cultural influence of a museum on modern art is derived not only from the collection of works of art and from the study courses and lectures held there, but more particularly from the creation of its own intellectual atmosphere in which the artist finds enrichment for his own work and ideas and in which the public can assimilate the artistic culture required by the mind of modern man."

The first building works were begun in December, 1954. The site on which the building is erected had been reclaimed from the sea only a short time previously when the municipal administration carried into effect a large-scale town-planning project, during the initial stages of which a long, broad strip along the coast was filled in. New roads built through this area are intended to improve traffic conditions in the town. This new land is also to be the site of a large public park surrounding the museum. Commanding a splendid view over Guanabara Bay and set in front of the city skyline, with the mountains rising in the background, the position is one of exceptional beauty and yet within easy reach of the inner city.

The plans reveal a tendency to harmonize the architecture with the background, stressing the horizontal in contrast with the undulating line of the mountains. A notable feature of the design of the main building is the series of external frames, joined by longitudinal beams, providing a means of both suspension and support for the floors. Apart from the entrance hall, the ground floor is completely free so that the view of the sea is practically uninterrupted.

The plan is a radical departure from the conventional idea that exhibitions call for closed galleries. There are no large walls and partitions. The whole interior of the exhibition galleries is visible from outside. The argument that visitors can concentrate better on the works of art only if the gallery is completely enclosed has been discounted. As is well known, the attention of a person confronted by a large number of works of art wanes rapidly unless there is an opportunity to rest the eyes and refresh the mind.

Variety in the organization of the room, large windows affording an uninterrupted view outside, and a thoughtful arrangement of the exhibits and showcases prevent rapid fatigue, and the viewer remains responsive to the impressions he receives.

Lighting also has its effect on the frame of mind in which the visitor views the works of art. Requirements as to the lighting of an art gallery are not restricted simply to the optimum illumination of the objects displayed. The light must also create a psychological atmosphere conducive to leisurely contemplation.

If it were merely a question of providing uniform lighting, artificial illumination would provide the best solution. From a psychological point of view, however, artificial light cannot satisfy the human need for variation because it is absolutely constant. On the other hand, natural light changes from one minute to the next, always affording new impressions.

Artificial lighting is indispensable at night and also for illuminating objects like drawings and textiles which are sensitive to sunlight. What form of artificial lighting should be chosen: incandescent bulbs, fluorescent tubes, or a combination of the two? The light of incandescent bulbs contains a high percentage of red and orange which alter the appearance of certain colors, whereas fluorescent tubes give a cold impression besides altering some colors. A proper combination of the two will therefore come very close to natural sunlight.

Another question arises in connection with natural lighting. Should the light come from above or from the side? Again, a combination of the two seems advisable. Certain objects are best illuminated from above, others from the side, while others show to greatest advantage in artificial light. An art gallery must be designed so that there is flexibility in the lighting and partitioning of the room. Large galleries are required, but small rooms are also needed for certain exhibits which call for a more intimate atmosphere.

The plans for the exhibition rooms of the museum are based on these considerations.

The large gallery measures 427 x 85 ft. and is entirely free from pillars, so that the floor areas may be used without restriction for the display of exhibits. A section with a ceiling clearance of 26 ft. is provided for large objects. The normal height of the rooms is 12 ft. The lower section is lighted from the side, while the higher part receives light from a saw-tooth roof 164 ft. long which is glazed with thermolux glass, and from safety glass domes in the roof fitted with thermolux reflectors.

The artificial lighting is of the mixed type. General lighting is by means of fluorescent tubes behind vinyl sheets which are secured to the ceiling and produce a diffusion of the light. This luminous surface is broken at intervals of 6 ft. 1/2 in. by transverse channels containing bulb reflectors with adjustable lenses. The reflectors can be directed as required at various points without dazzling visitors.

The windows of the gallery are oriented north and south. Sun screening is of minor importance on the south façade, since this side is exposed to direct sunlight only during a short period in summer under conditions which readily permit protection. The north façade, however, is exposed to the sun for most of the year. Adequate screening was necessary to prevent high temperatures in the interior as a result of the sunlight falling directly on the façade. Even with an air-conditioning plant, screening is still necessary for economy. For this reason, broad longitudinal beams were fitted so that they would rest on the external angles of the reinforced concrete ribs. However, there are periods during the winter solstice when this protection is not adequate. These windows were therefore glazed with thermolux and provided with aluminum blinds which permit the amount of light entering the room to be controlled.

The pillars supporting the framework of the building had to be sunk 66 ft. deep in the earth because of the foundation soil. The reinforced concrete ribs forming the frame of the structure are placed at intervals of 32 ft. 12 in. and have a ground span of 85 ft. Each rib bifurcates at ground level. The inwardly inclined struts take the load of the first upper story, whereas the outwardly inclined struts carry the crossbeams from which the second story and the roof platforms are suspended by means of tension rods.

Annexed to the gallery building at the western end is a U-shaped structure arranged around a garden courtyard and containing studios, a restaurant, administration and storage rooms, and other ancillary installations for the museum. Access to the exhibition galleries, the administrative offices, and the studios is gained through the central section of the gallery building.

The visitor passes to the exhibition rooms through a hall on the ground floor in which are located the ticket office, cloakrooms, inquiry office, lavatories, and a booth, also accessible from outside, in which publications are sold.

A broad, round staircase leads to the gallery, which occupies the whole of the first upper story and part of the second. At the west end of the gallery story, there are passenger and freight elevators, toilet facilities, entrances to the restaurant, and, on the second floor, offices. At the east end, a terrace joins the main building to the theater. On the upper floor there are, apart from the section reserved for exhibitions, an auditorium seating 200 persons, a projection room and foyer, a library with a reading room and a book store, small projection rooms for films and slides, a record library, etc. Provision has also been made for storing pictures not on exhibit. The air-conditioning plant creates optimum conditions for preserving stored works of art.

Storerooms and ancillary installations are accommodated partly on the ground floor and partly in the cellar of the administrative wing. The approach road for trucks lies on the west side of this building. By means of an electrically operated gate 16 ft. high, the vehicles can approach a ramp inside the building which is arranged at the level of the truck platform.

Here goods are received and dispatched, and incoming goods can be stored. Cases are handled with the aid of a derrick and transported by conveyer belt from the truck to the packing room, where they are opened and the contents inspected and booked. The articles are then passed either to the photo studio and then to the storeroom, or directly to the preparation room in which all exhibits are collected. Empty cases are forwarded by conveyer belt to the cellar. The cellar also contains workshops for joiners, fitters, electricians, plumbers, painters, and others; a storage room for sculpture and other objects; a disinfection room with a gas chamber for the destruction of insects and parasites; and also the air-conditioning plant, electric installations, fire-protection devices, water tanks, rubbish collection, and so forth.

The single-story part of the building to the south, on the opposite side of the inner courtyard, accommodates studios and work and lecture rooms for painting, plastic and graphic arts, ceramics, etc. Its roof is designed as a garden terrace which is arranged to encircle the entire administration wing on the first upper floor.

Aerial view of Guanabara Bay. In the foreground on the right can be seen the filled-in strip of coastland with the site for the museum.
Luftansicht der Guanabara-Bucht. Im Vordergrund rechts der aufgeschüttete Küstenstreifen mit dem Museumsgelände.

Museum für moderne Kunst, Rio de Janeiro
begonnen 1954

Statik: Serviços de engentraria Emílio Baumgart und Escritorio tecnico da Companhia Construtora Nacional S.A.

Der Aufgabenbereich dieses Museums beschränkt sich nicht nur auf Kunstausstellungen und Vorträge. Es bestand vielmehr die Absicht, ein Kunstzentrum zu entwickeln, das aus dem eigentlichen Museum, einer Schule mit Vortrags- und Arbeitsräumen und einem Theater für 1000 Personen besteht, das für Schauspiele, Konzerte, Balletts, Filmvorführungen und Tagungen dienen soll.

Die folgenden Ausführungen sind einem Aufsatz des Architekten entnommen. Er zitiert zunächst die Einführungsworte, mit denen das Museum im Januar 1954 die vorläufigen Pläne für sein neues Gebäude veröffentlichte:

»Der kulturelle Einfluß eines Museums für moderne Kunst entsteht nicht nur durch die Sammlung von Kunstwerken und die Kurse und Vorträge, die gehalten werden, sondern vor allem durch die Schaffung eines eigenen geistigen Klimas, in dem der Künstler Bereicherung für sein Werk und Denken findet, und in dem das Publikum die künstlerische Kultur in sich aufnehmen kann, die der moderne Geist erfordert.«

Im Dezember 1954 begannen die ersten Bauarbeiten. Das Gelände, auf dem die Anlage errichtet wird, war erst kurz zuvor dem Meer abgewonnen worden, als die Stadtverwaltung ein Stadtplanungsprojekt großen Umfangs ausführte, das mit der Aufschüttung eines langen und breiten Streifens an der Küste begann. Neue Straßen, die durch dieses Gebiet gelegt werden, sollen die Verkehrsverhältnisse der Stadt verbessern. Außerdem soll auf dem neuen Gelände ein ausgedehnter öffentlicher Park angelegt werden, der das Museum umgibt. Die Lage — mit dem großartigen Blick über die Guanabara-Bucht, vor der Stadtsilhouette und den sich im Hintergrund erhebenden Bergen — ist außerordentlich schön, zudem läßt sich das Museum von der Innenstadt her leicht erreichen.

Der Entwurf zeigt die Tendenz, die Architektur mit dem Hintergrund in Einklang zu bringen, daher die Betonung der Horizontalen im Kontrast zu den welligen Linienzügen der Berge. Bemerkenswert an der Konstruktion des Hauptgebäudes ist die Aufhängung beziehungsweise Unterstützung der Geschoßebenen durch eine Reihe von außen liegenden Rahmen, die durch Längsträger miteinander verbunden sind. Das Erdgeschoß bleibt, abgesehen von der Eingangshalle,

vollkommen frei, so daß der Blick auf das Meer kaum unterbrochen wird.

Der Entwurf weicht vollkommen von der konventionellen Auffassung ab, die für Ausstellungen geschlossene Galerien fordert. Es gibt hier keine großen Wände und Trennungen. Das gesamte Innere der Ausstellungsgalerien ist von außen sichtbar. Das Argument, eine Ausstellungsgalerie solle durch absolute Geschlossenheit die Bedingungen schaffen, die eine bessere Konzentration des Besuchers erlauben, wird nicht anerkannt. Wie man weiß, läßt die Aufmerksamkeit eines Menschen, der sich einer großen Zahl von Kunstwerken gegenübersieht, schnell nach, solange nicht eine Möglichkeit besteht, das Auge auszuruhen und sich zu erholen.

Abwechslungsreiche Gliederung des Raumes, große Fensterflächen, die den Blick nach draußen freigeben, und überlegte Anordnung von Ausstellungsobjekten und Schaukästen verhindern eine rasche Ermüdung und befähigen den Beschauer, den Eindrücken gegenüber empfänglich zu bleiben.

Auch die Belichtung hat einen Einfluß auf die Verfassung des Besuchers. Die Anforderungen, die an die Belichtung einer Kunstgalerie gestellt werden müssen, beschränken sich nicht nur auf die beste Beleuchtung der ausgestellten Objekte. Das Licht soll außerdem ein psychisches Klima schaffen, das den Besucher dazu einlädt, sich mit Muße der Betrachtung hinzugeben.

Wenn es sich nur darum handeln würde, eine gleichmäßige Belichtung zu erreichen, wäre künstliches Licht die beste Lösung. Psychologisch gesehen, ist jedoch das künstliche Licht nicht geeignet, dem menschlichen Bedürfnis nach Variation entgegenzukommen. Es ist vollkommen gleichbleibend, während natürliches Licht

durch seinen lebendigen Wechsel von Minute zu Minute neue Eindrücke schafft.

Künstliche Belichtung ist nachts unerläßlich, und auch zur Beleuchtung von Objekten, die gegen Sonnenlicht empfindlich sind, wie Zeichnungen und Stoffe. Welche Art von künstlichem Licht soll man nun wählen? Glühlampen oder Leuchtstoffröhren oder eine Kombination von beiden? Glühlampenlicht enthält einen hohen Prozentsatz von Rot- und Orangestrahlen, die das Aussehen bestimmter Farben verändern, während Leuchtstoffröhren einen kalten Eindruck vermitteln und ebenfalls einige Farben verändern. Doch wird eine richtige Kombination von beiden dem natürlichen Sonnenlicht sehr nahekommen.

Ferner ist die Frage der natürlichen Belichtung zu untersuchen. Deckenlicht oder Seitenlicht? Es erscheint auch hier ratsam, eine Kombination zu wählen. Bestimmte Objekte werden am besten von oben belichtet, andere von der Seite, andere wiederum durch Kunstlicht. Eine Kunstgalerie muß so gestaltet werden, daß eine Flexibilität in der Behandlung des Lichtes und in der Raumaufteilung möglich ist. Es sind große Galerien erforderlich, aber oft auch kleine Räume für bestimmte Objekte, die eine intimere Atmosphäre brauchen.

Diese Überlegungen liegen dem Entwurf für die Ausstellungsräume des Museums zugrunde.

Die große Galerie mißt 130 x 26 m und ist vollkommen frei von Stützen, so daß die Geschoßflächen uneingeschränkt für die Anordnung der Ausstellungsobjekte zur Verfügung stehen. Für besonders große Objekte ist ein Teil mit einer lichten Höhe von 8 m vorgesehen. Die normale Geschoßhöhe beträgt 3.60 m. Der niedrigere Abschnitt ist seitlich belichtet, der höhere durch ein Shed von 50 m Länge mit Thermoluxglas und durch

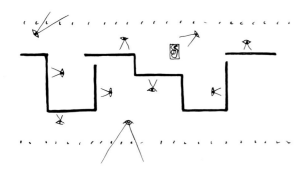

The unrestricted gallery: external walls of glass; light, easily moved partition walls which can be arranged as required.
Der unbegrenzte Galerieraum: Außenwände aus Glas; leichte, bewegliche Stellwände in beliebiger Aufstellung.

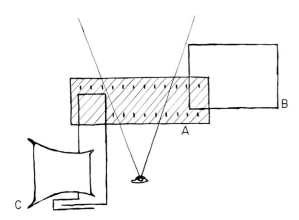

Site sketch: The exhibition gallery (A) lies between the administrative structure (B) and the theater (C). It is built in such a way as to allow visitors an uninterrupted view of the sea through the open ground floor.
Lageskizze. Die Ausstellungsgalerie (A) liegt zwischen dem Verwaltungstrakt (B) und dem Theater (C). Sie ist so konstruiert, daß die Besucher durch das freie Erdgeschoß ungehindert auf das Meer sehen.

eine Anzahl von Plexiglaskuppeln im Dach mit Thermoluxreflektoren.

Das künstliche Licht ist gemischt. Die Allgemeinbeleuchtung geschieht durch Leuchtstoffröhren hinter Vinyl-Platten, die an der Decke befestigt sind und eine Lichtstreuung bewirken. Diese leuchtende Fläche ist in Abständen von zwei Metern durch Querkanäle unterbrochen, die Glühlampenreflektoren mit verstellbaren Linsen aufnehmen. Die Reflektoren können den Erfordernissen entsprechend auf bestimmte Punkte gerichtet werden, ohne die Besucher zu blenden.

Die Fenster der Galerie sind nach Süden und Norden gerichtet. Auf der Südfront spielt der Sonnenschutz eine geringere Rolle, da diese Seite nicht der direkten Bestrahlung ausgesetzt ist, mit Ausnahme einer kurzen Periode im Sommer, jedoch unter Bedingungen, die leicht einen Schutz ermöglichen. Die Nordfront ist jedoch für die längste Zeit des Jahres der Sonne ausgesetzt. Um das Entstehen hoher Innentemperaturen durch das direkt auf die Fassade fallende Sonnenlicht zu verhindern, war eine ausreichende Abschirmung notwendig. Selbst mit einer Klimaanlage kann aus ökonomischen Gründen auf eine derartige Abschirmung nicht verzichtet werden. Es wurden deshalb breite Längsträger angebracht, die auf den Außenwinkeln der Stahlbetonrippen ruhen. Dennoch gibt es während der Wintersonnenwende Perioden, in denen dieser Schutz nicht ausreicht. Diese Fenster wurden daher mit Thermolux verglast und mit Aluminiumjalousien versehen, die eine Regulierung der eindringenden Lichtmenge ermöglichen.

Die Pfeiler, auf denen das Rahmenwerk des Gebäudes errichtet wurde, mußten wegen der Beschaffenheit des Baugrundes bis zu 20 m tief in die Erde gesenkt werden. Die das Rahmenwerk bildenden Stahlbetonrippen haben Abstände von 10 m und eine Bodenspannweite von 26 m. In Terrainhöhe gabelt sich jede Rippe. Die nach innen geneigten Streben nehmen den Druck des ersten Obergeschosses auf, und die nach außen geneigten stützen die Querbalken, an denen mit Zugstäben das zweite Obergeschoß und die Dachplattformen aufgehängt sind.

Im Westen schließt sich an das Galeriegebäude ein U-förmig um einen Gartenhof gelegter Trakt mit Studios, Restaurant, Verwaltungs- und Lagerräumen und sonstigen Hilfseinrichtungen für das Museum an. Der Zugang zu den Ausstellungsgalerien, den Verwaltungsbüros und den Studios führt durch den Mittelabschnitt des Galeriegebäudes.

Der Besucher erreicht die Ausstellungsräume durch eine Halle im Erdgeschoß, in der sich Kasse, Garderobe, Auskunft, Toiletten und ein auch von außen zu-

gänglicher Kiosk zum Verkauf von Publikationen befinden.

Über eine breite runde Treppe gelangt man zur Galerie, die das ganze erste Obergeschoß und einen Teil des zweiten einnimmt. Am westlichen Ende des Galeriegeschosses befinden sich Personen- und Lastenaufzüge, Toiletteneinrichtungen, die Eingänge zum Restaurant und im zweiten Obergeschoß die Büros. Am östlichen Ende verbindet eine Terrasse das Hauptgebäude mit dem Theater. Im Obergeschoß befindet sich außer dem für Ausstellungen reservierten Abschnitt ein Auditorium mit 200 Plätzen, Projektionsraum und Foyer, eine Bibliothek einschließlich Leseraum und Büchermagazin, kleine Projektionsräume für Filme und Diapositive, eine Discothek usw. Ferner ist ein Aufbewahrungsraum für nicht ausgestellte Bilder vorgesehen. Eine Klimaanlage schafft optimale Bedingungen für die Erhaltung der aufbewahrten Werke.

Lagerräume und Hilfseinrichtungen sind teils im Erdgeschoß, teils im Keller des Verwaltungsflügels untergebracht. Die Zufahrt für Lastwagen liegt auf der Westseite dieses Gebäudes. Durch ein elektrisch bedientes 5 m hohes Tor können die Fahrzeuge im Innern des Baukörpers an eine Rampe heranfahren, deren Höhe der Ladefläche von Lastwagen entspricht.

Hier befinden sich Empfang und Abfertigung sowie ein Lager für angekommene Güter. Die Kisten werden mit Hilfe eines Ladebaumes und eines Förderbandes vom Lastwagen bis zum Packraum gebracht, wo sie geöffnet werden und der Inhalt geprüft und gebucht wird. Danach führt der Weg entweder zum Fotostudio und dann zum Lagerraum oder direkt zum Vorbereitungsraum, in dem alle Ausstellungsobjekte gesammelt werden. Die leeren Kisten werden mit einem Transportband in den Keller befördert. Ebenfalls im Keller liegen die Werkstätten für Schreiner, Schlosser, Elektriker, Klempner, Maler und andere, ein Aufbewahrungsraum für Skulpturen und andere Objekte, ein Desinfektionsraum mit einer Gaskammer für die Vernichtung von Insekten und Parasiten, ferner die Klimaanlage, elektrische Installationen und Feuerschutzeinrichtungen, Wassertanks, Abfallplatz und so weiter.

Der eingeschossige südliche Gebäudeteil, auf der gegenüber liegenden Seite des Innenhofes, nimmt die Studios, Arbeits- und Vortragsräume für Malerei, Plastik, Graphik, Keramik und so weiter auf. Seine Decke ist als Gartenterrasse ausgebildet, die im ersten Obergeschoß um den ganzen Verwaltungsflügel herumgeführt wird.

An ideal site in the center of the city, on a strip of land reclaimed from the sea, surrounded by a large public park. The inland side overlooks the city and mountains, the other side commands a splendid view of Guanabara Bay.
Ideale städtebauliche Situation im Herzen der Stadt auf angeschüttetem Küstenstreifen, umgeben von einem ausgedehnten öffentlichen Park. Auf der Landseite Stadt- und Bergsilhouette, zum Meer hin großartiger Blick über die Guanabara-Bucht.

A large portion of the site is left free, permitting uninterrupted extension of the park area to the sea. The ground floor below the gallery is a lounge, open on all sides.
Da ein großer Teil der Bodenfläche freigelassen ist, können sich die Gartenanlagen unter dem Gebäude hindurch bis ans Meer erstrecken. Im Erdgeschoß unter der Ausstellungsgalerie eine nach allen Seiten offene Wandelhalle.

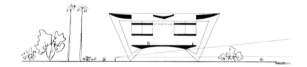

Unique constructional features: Frame consisting of concrete ribs with a ground span of 85 ft., placed at intervals of 32 ft. 12 in.; the interior is free from pillars, providing unbroken floor space measuring 427 x 85 ft. for displays; upper floors are suspended from the pillars of the frame construction; jutting roof and sheds give protection from the sun and make air circulation possible; color and texture of rough concrete are used for artistic expression; materials and form are components in the total architectural conception.
Konstruktive Merkmale: Rahmenwerk aus Stahlbetonrippen mit 26 m Spannweite in 10 m Abstand; Inneres frei von Stützen, ununterbrochene Geschoßflächen von 130 x 26 m für Ausstellungszwecke, Obergeschosse vom Deckenträger der Rahmenkonstruktion abgehängt; vorspringende Deckenplatte und Sheds als Sonnenschutz und Belüftungsmöglichkeit; Farbe und Struktur des schalungsrauhen Betons als formales Ausdrucksmittel; Einbeziehung der Konstruktion als Element einer plastischen Gesamtkonzeption.

Photomontage with a model of the museum. View of the bay and ▷ Sugar Loaf Mountain. The surrounding park is laid out according to the designs of Roberto Burle-Marx.
Photomontage mit dem Modell des Museums. Blick auf Bucht und Zuckerhut. Das umgebende Parkgelände wird nach Entwürfen von Roberto Burle-Marx angelegt.

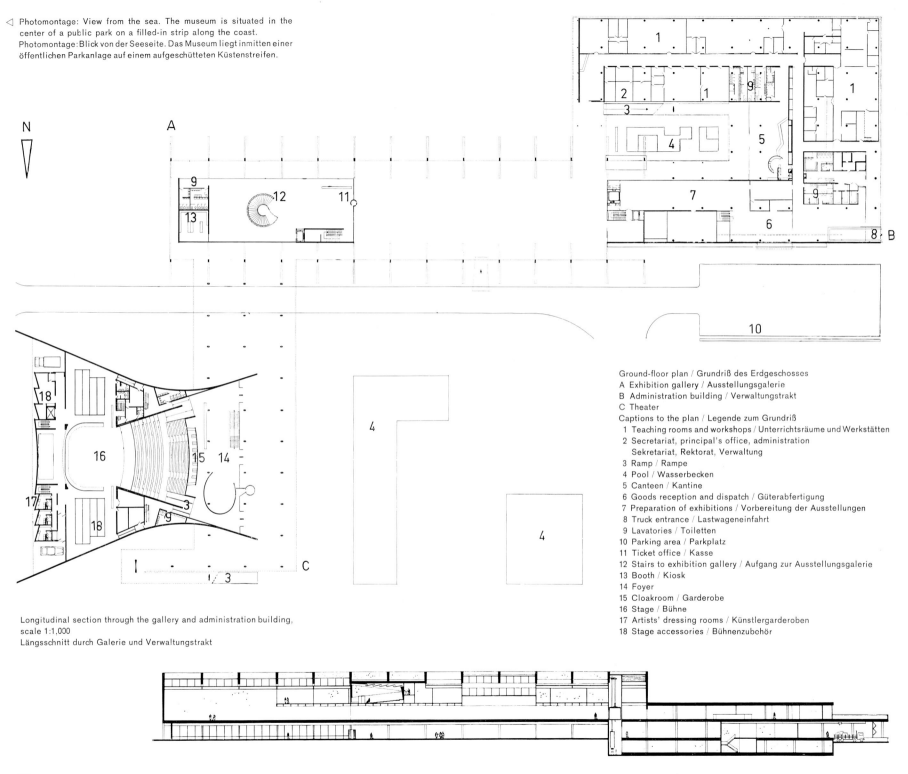

◁ Photomontage: View from the sea. The museum is situated in the center of a public park on a filled-in strip along the coast.
Photomontage: Blick von der Seeseite. Das Museum liegt inmitten einer öffentlichen Parkanlage auf einem aufgeschütteten Küstenstreifen.

Longitudinal section through the gallery and administration building, scale 1:1,000
Längsschnitt durch Galerie und Verwaltungstrakt

Ground-floor plan / Grundriß des Erdgeschosses
A Exhibition gallery / Ausstellungsgalerie
B Administration building / Verwaltungstrakt
C Theater
Captions to the plan / Legende zum Grundriß
1 Teaching rooms and workshops / Unterrichtsräume und Werkstätten
2 Secretariat, principal's office, administration
   Sekretariat, Rektorat, Verwaltung
3 Ramp / Rampe
4 Pool / Wasserbecken
5 Canteen / Kantine
6 Goods reception and dispatch / Güterabfertigung
7 Preparation of exhibitions / Vorbereitung der Ausstellungen
8 Truck entrance / Lastwageneinfahrt
9 Lavatories / Toiletten
10 Parking area / Parkplatz
11 Ticket office / Kasse
12 Stairs to exhibition gallery / Aufgang zur Ausstellungsgalerie
13 Booth / Kiosk
14 Foyer
15 Cloakroom / Garderobe
16 Stage / Bühne
17 Artists' dressing rooms / Künstlergarderoben
18 Stage accessories / Bühnenzubehör

71

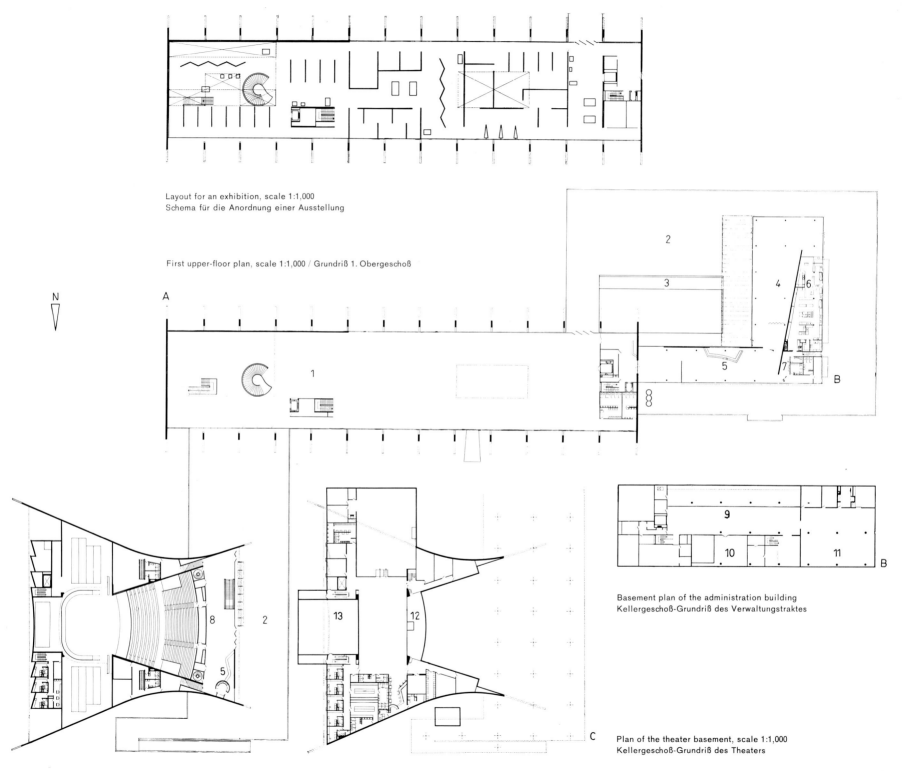

Layout for an exhibition, scale 1:1,000
Schema für die Anordnung einer Ausstellung

First upper-floor plan, scale 1:1,000 / Grundriß 1. Obergeschoß

N

A

B

Basement plan of the administration building
Kellergeschoß-Grundriß des Verwaltungstraktes

C

Plan of the theater basement, scale 1:1,000
Kellergeschoß-Grundriß des Theaters

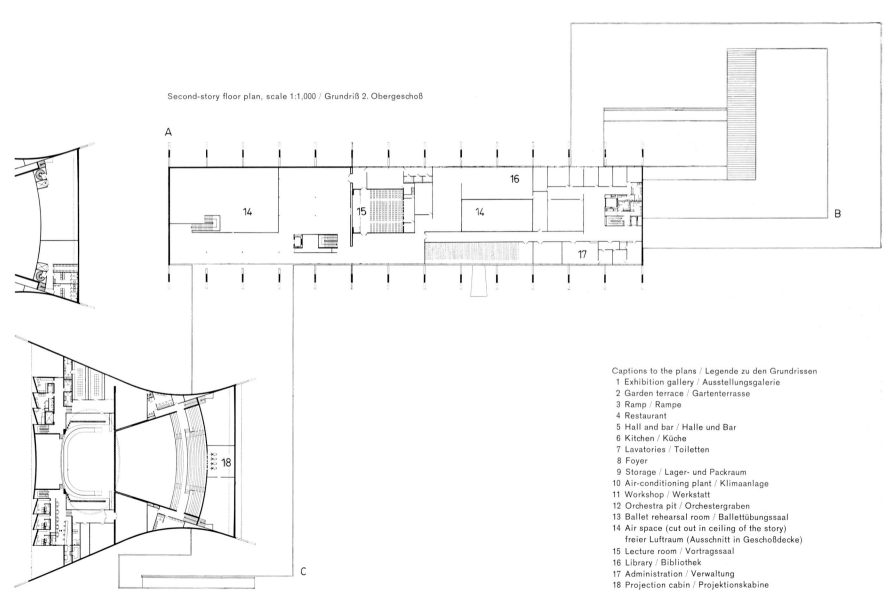

Second-story floor plan, scale 1:1,000 / Grundriß 2. Obergeschoß

A

B

C

14

15

16

14

17

18

Captions to the plans / Legende zu den Grundrissen
1 Exhibition gallery / Ausstellungsgalerie
2 Garden terrace / Gartenterrasse
3 Ramp / Rampe
4 Restaurant
5 Hall and bar / Halle und Bar
6 Kitchen / Küche
7 Lavatories / Toiletten
8 Foyer
9 Storage / Lager- und Packraum
10 Air-conditioning plant / Klimaanlage
11 Workshop / Werkstatt
12 Orchestra pit / Orchestergraben
13 Ballet rehearsal room / Ballettübungssaal
14 Air space (cut out in ceiling of the story)
   freier Luftraum (Ausschnitt in Geschoßdecke)
15 Lecture room / Vortragssaal
16 Library / Bibliothek
17 Administration / Verwaltung
18 Projection cabin / Projektionskabine

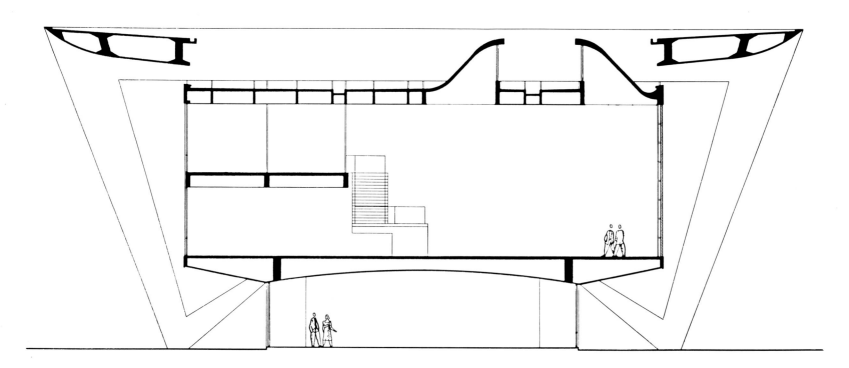

Cross-section through the east part of the gallery building,
scale 1:200
Querschnitt durch den Ostteil des Galeriegebäudes

Section through the ceiling of the exhibition gallery, scale 1:20
Schnitt durch die Decke der Ausstellungsgalerie
1 Floor / Fußboden
2 Reinforced concrete ceiling / Stahlbetondecke
3 Air-conditioning system / Klimaanlage
4 Fluorescent tubes / Leuchtstoffröhren
5 Reflector / Reflektor
6 Vinyl sheet / Vinylplatte

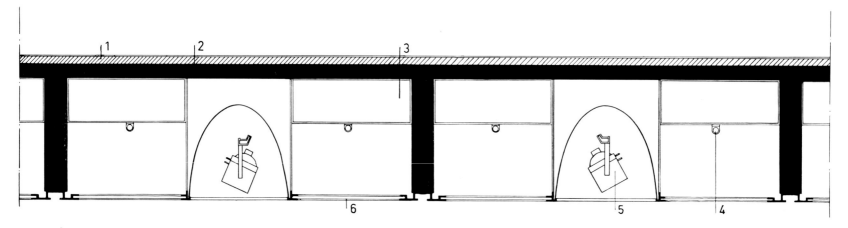

The central part of the gallery during construction.
Der mittlere Teil des Galeriegebäudes im Rohbau.

Private initiative has been responsible for the conception of the Rio Museum of Modern Art. Mrs. Niomar Moniz Sodré, its Executive Director since 1951, led a team of collaborators in transforming an institution of limited activity into a highly active center of art. The Museum was allowed the use of ground-floor space in the Ministry of Education and Health for a period of five years, until 1958. In 1954, construction of the new building began on a land area of 47,760 sq. yd. bestowed by the city. In January, 1958, a section of the building was completed, and the Museum staff moved into its own headquarters.

Das Museum für moderne Kunst entstand aus privater Initiative. An seiner Spitze steht Frau Niomar Moniz Sodré, seit 1951 Direktorin, die eine Institution von beschränkter Aktivität in ein weit wirkendes Kunstzentrum verwandelt hat. Zunächst stand dem Museum für fünf Jahre das Erdgeschoß des Ministeriums für Erziehung und Gesundheit zur Verfügung (bis 1958). Im Jahr 1954 wurde der Grundstein für das neue Kunstzentrum gelegt, für das die Stadt dem Museum ein Grundstück von 40 000 qm übereignet hatte. Im Januar 1958 konnte der erste Teilabschnitt, der künftige Verwaltungstrakt, eingeweiht werden, so daß die Mitarbeiter des Museums nun im eigenen Hause untergebracht sind.

Reinforcement design for the frame of the gallery building, scale 1:200
Armierungsplan der Rahmenkonstruktion für das Galeriegebäude

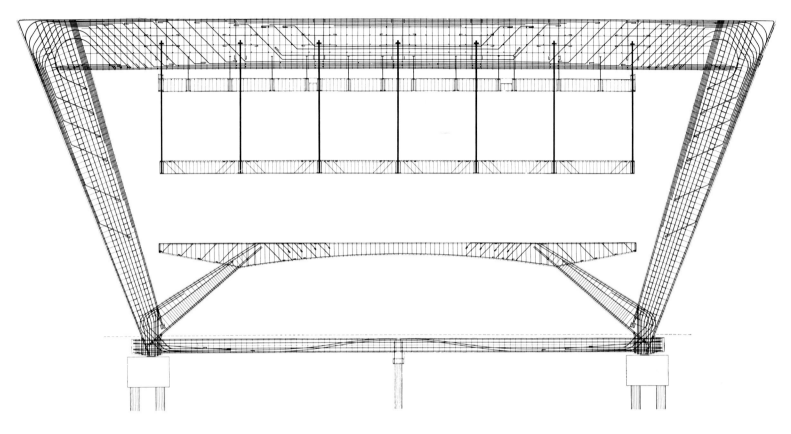

Skeleton of the frame construction of the gallery.
Die Rahmenkonstruktion des Galeriegebäudes im Rohbau.

The reinforcement of the pillars.
Armierung der Deckenträger.

View from the east into the upper floors of the gallery building. The ▷
second story is suspended by means of tension rods.
Blick vom Ostteil des ersten Obergeschosses in das Innere des
Galeriegebäudes. In der Mitte das an Zugstäben aufgehängte zweite
Obergeschoß.

The ground-floor of the gallery building is completely free. A broad
semicircular staircase leads the visitors to the exhibition rooms.
Blick in die offene Erdgeschoßhalle des Galeriegebäudes. Die Besucher erreichen die Ausstellungsräume über die halbkreisförmig
geschwungene Treppe.

View of the gallery building from the south showing the framework
with the floor areas which are free from pillars. The bifurcated reinforced concrete ribs are placed at intervals of 32 ft. 12 in. and have
a ground span of 85 ft.
Südansicht der Ausstellungsgalerie. Im Rahmenwerk des Gebäudes
die stützenfreien Geschoßplatten. Die gegabelten Stahlbetonrippen
haben Abstände von 10 m und eine Bodenspannweite von 26 m.

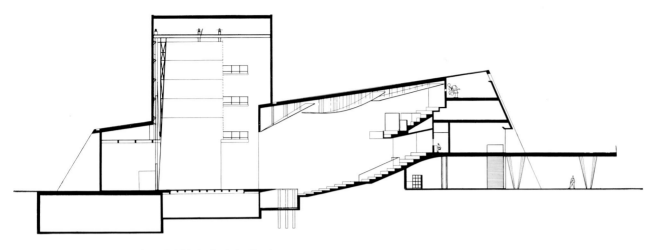

Section through the theater, scale 1:500 / Schnitt durch das Theater

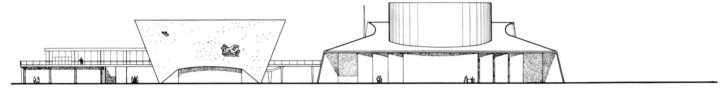

View from the east, scale 1:1,000 / Ostansicht

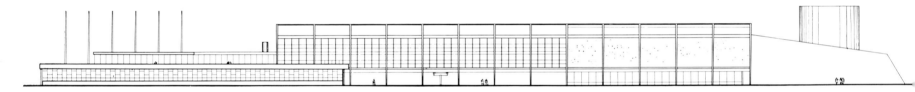

View from the south, scale 1:1,000 / Südansicht

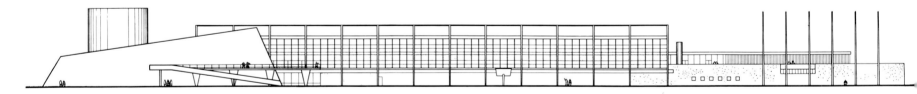

View from the north, scale 1:1,000 / Nordansicht

View from the west, scale 1:1,000 / Westansicht

80

The theater will seat 1,000 persons. The stage area is 164 ft. wide; the proscenium arch, which is 39 ft., can be widened to 52 ft. for symphony concerts. The height of the proscenium arch is 23 ft. and the height to the gridiron 59 ft. The stage is 66 ft. deep, and 43 ft. when the cyclorama is lowered. The side scenes, which are mounted on frames and rails, can be moved laterally and backward by centrally controlled electric motors. There are four independent units at each side and one at the back. A wide variety of combinations and a rapid change of scene are thus possible without dismounting the side scenes. To improve the acoustics during concerts, movable sound walls can be fitted. The large orchestra pit with an area of 861 sq. ft. can be raised to the level of the auditorium. As soon as the curtain rises, the doors of the auditorium are automatically locked. Late-comers can hear the performance transmitted by means of loud-speakers in the vestibule. The front part of the building contains a covered approach and hall on the ground floor; a foyer on the upper floor gives access to the garden terrace, which connects the theater with the top floor of the gallery.

Das Theater hat 1000 Sitzplätze. Der Bühnenraum ist 50 m breit, die Bühnenöffnung 12 m; für Symphoniekonzerte kann sie auf 16 m erweitert werden. Die Höhe des Bühnenausschnitts beträgt 7 m, die Höhe bis zum Schnürboden 18 m. Der Bühnenraum ist 20 m tief, bei herabgelassenem Rundhorizont 13 m. Die Kulissen werden auf Schienen und Rahmen geführt. Sie sind durch zentral gesteuerte Elektromotoren seitlich und nach hinten verschiebbar. An den Seiten stehen je vier voneinander unabhängige Einheiten, im Hintergrund eine Einheit zur Verfügung. Dadurch werden vielseitige Kombinationen und ein rascher Szenenwechsel ohne Abbau der Kulissen ermöglicht. Um die akustischen Verhältnisse zu verbessern, werden bei Konzerten bewegliche Schallwände angebracht. Der 80 qm große Orchestergraben kann auf die Höhe des Auditoriums gehoben werden. Sobald sich der Vorhang hebt, schließen sich automatisch die Türen des Zuschauerraums. Zuspätkommende können die Aufführung bei Lautsprecherübertragung durch Scheiben im Vorraum verfolgen. Der Vorbau enthält im Erdgeschoß eine gedeckte Zufahrt und Halle, im Obergeschoß das Foyer, von dem aus die Gartenterrasse betreten werden kann, die das Theater mit dem Hauptgeschoß der Galerie verbindet.

Garden plan for the surroundings of the museum.
Design by Roberto Burle-Marx.
Gartenplan für die Umgebung des Museums.
Entwurf Roberto Burle-Marx.

Inner courtyards of the administration block, which has now been completed. On the left, the structure with the studios.
Innenhof des inzwischen fertiggestellten Verwaltungstraktes.
Links der Trakt mit den Studios.

The terrace in front of the future restaurant in the upper story of
the administration building, covered with a sun-screen lattice.
Die mit einem Sonnenschutzgitter überdeckte Terrasse vor dem
künftigen Restaurant im Obergeschoß des Verwaltungstraktes.

Page / Seite 84
Until the gallery building is completed, the upper story of the administration building is to be used as an exhibition room. View looking
into the interior from the covered terrace.
Das Obergeschoß des Verwaltungstraktes dient bis zur Fertigstellung
des Galeriegebäudes als Ausstellungsraum. Blick von der überdeckten
Terrasse ins Innere.

Page / Seite 85
Provisional exhibition room. Here, too, the principles of side light,
and an uninterrupted view through large windows have been main-
tained.
Der provisorische Ausstellungsraum. Auch hier Seitenlicht und freier
Blick durch große Fensterflächen.

Residence for Carmen Portinho,
Rio de Janeiro – 1950/52

This dwelling house designed for the woman director of the municipal housing office in Rio de Janeiro lies outside the town in the mountains. The garage and maid's room are arranged flush with the ground on the mountainside. Following the slope of the terrain, the open patio looks over the valley. Sloping ramps on either side lead to the main section, which stands on pillars at an angle to the slope. The actual living quarters therefore project a good distance over the slope, thus obviating unnecessary site leveling.
Pleasant cross-ventilation is provided by the upper part of a living room and bedroom wall which permits the passage of air. The large, fully glazed wall of the living room affords a splendid view of the luxuriant vegetation near the house and of the landscape stretching away into the distance.

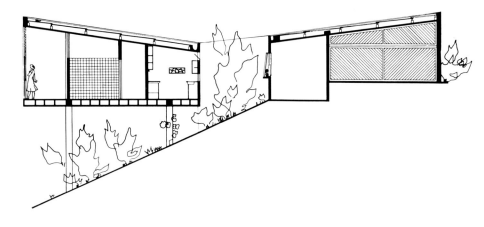

Longitudinal section, scale 1:200 / Längsschnitt

Wohnhaus für Carmen Portinho,
Rio de Janeiro – 1950/52

Dieses Wohnhaus für die Direktorin des städtischen Amtes für Wohnungsbau in Rio de Janeiro liegt außerhalb der Stadt in den Bergen. Garage und Mädchenzimmer wurden auf der Bergseite ebenerdig angelegt. Zum Tal hin schließt sich der offene Patio an, der dem abfallenden Gelände folgt. Auf beiden Seiten führen Verbindungsrampen zu dem quer zum Hang gestellten, auf Pilotis stehenden Hauptteil. Dadurch ragt der eigentliche Wohntrakt weit über den Abhang hinaus und zugleich wurden unnötige Erdbewegungen vermieden.
Da der obere Teil einer Wohnraum- und Schlafraumwand luftdurchlässig ist, kommt eine angenehme Querlüftung zustande. Die große Glaswand des Wohnraumes bietet eine großartige Aussicht auf die reiche Vegetation dicht beim Haus und auf die sich in der Ferne ausdehnende Landschaft.

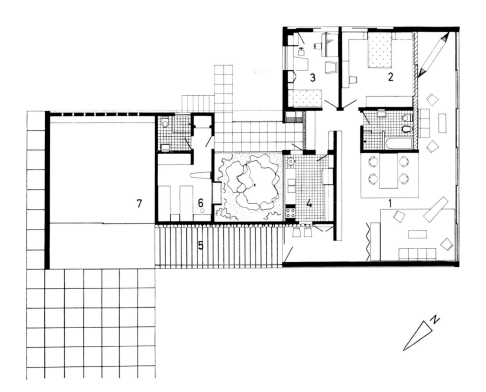

Floor plan, scale 1:200 / Grundriß
1 Living room / Wohnraum
2 Bedroom / Schlafraum
3 Work room / Arbeitsraum
4 Kitchen / Küche
5 Ramp / Rampe
6 Maid's room / Mädchenzimmer
7 Garage

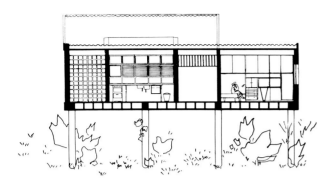 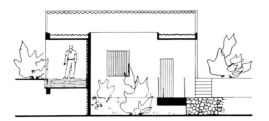 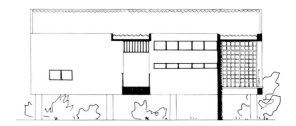

Cross-sections, scale 1:200 / Querschnitte

The section containing the garage and maid's room on the mountain-side. On the right, the connecting ramp to the main building.
Der bergseitige Bauteil mit Garage und Mädchenzimmer.
Rechts die Verbindungsrampe zum Haupttrakt.

View of the main part of the house seen from the valley side. The surrounding vegetation has been fully integrated with the house.
Ansicht des Hauptteils von der Talseite. Völlige Einbindung in die umgebende Vegetation.

Side view. On the left, the obliquely arranged main part of the house. On the right, the section on the mountainside with maid's room and garage.
Seitenansicht. Links der quergestellte Hauptteil. Rechts der bergseitige Trakt mit Mädchenzimmer und Garage.

The main part of the house projects far out over the slope on pillars.
Pilotis heben den Hauptteil weit über den Hang hinaus.

The glazed wall of the large living room.
Die Fensterwand des großen Wohnraumes.

House for Dr. Couto e Silva, Rio de Janeiro – 1953/55

This house is situated at Tijuca, a residential quarter of Rio de Janeiro in a mountainous region which has an excellent climate and is within easy reach of the city center. It is a favorite site for weekend houses and a place of retreat during the hot summer.

The building program was divided into three levels so as to take advantage of the irregular terrain. Bedrooms, bathroom, showers, lavatories, and a study are placed at the very top. Next, at a somewhat lower level, is the living room, which opens to the inner portion of the site and the utility rooms. There is a swimming pool in the garden at the same level as the upper rooms. An open garage is arranged below the bedrooms.

In the portion of the site ascending to the rear, a flight of steps leads to a small summer house containing a workshop and the caretaker's apartment.

The designs for the garden and the blue-white-brown ceramic wall at the front are by Roberto Burle-Marx.

Haus für Dr. Couto e Silva, Rio de Janeiro – 1953/55

Dieses Haus liegt in Tijuca, einem Wohnviertel von Rio de Janeiro in bergiger Gegend mit ausgezeichnetem Klima und nicht weit vom Stadtzentrum. Es ist ein bevorzugtes Gebiet für Wochenendhäuser und ein Zufluchtsort besonders während der sommerlichen Hitzeperiode.

Unter Ausnutzung des unregelmäßigen Geländes wurde das Bauprogramm auf drei Ebenen verteilt. Ganz oben befinden sich Schlafräume, Bad, Duschen, Toiletten und ein Arbeitszimmer. Daneben, etwas tiefer, liegt der Wohnraum, der sich zum inneren Teil des Grundstücks hin öffnet, und die Wirtschaftsräume. Auf gleichem Niveau mit den oberen Räumen ist im Garten ein Schwimmbad angelegt. Unter den Schlafräumen befindet sich eine offene Garage.

In dem nach hinten ansteigenden Teil des Grundstücks führt eine Treppe zu einem kleineren Gartenhaus, das ein Atelier und die Hausmeisterwohnung enthält.

Die Entwürfe für die Gartenanlage und die blau-weißbraune Keramikwand an der Vorderfront stammen von Roberto Burle-Marx.

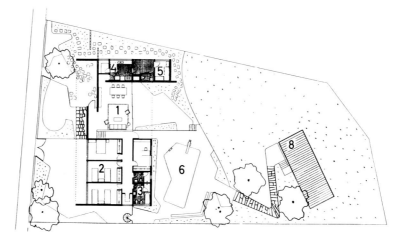

Ground-floor plan, scale 1:500
Grundriß Erdgeschoß

Street front, with open garage.
Straßenfront mit offener Garage.

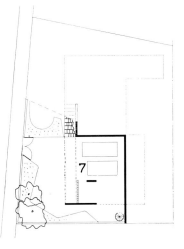

Captions to the plans / Legende zu den Grundrissen
1 Living room / Wohnraum
2 Bedrooms / Schlafräume
3 Bath / Bad
4 Kitchen / Küche
5 Staff room / Personalzimmer
6 Swimming pool / Schwimmbad
7 Garage
8 Summer house / Gartenhaus

Floor plan of basement, scale 1:500
Grundriß Untergeschoß

Over-all view from the street side.
Gesamtansicht von der Straßenseite.

The swimming pool in the garden, on the living-room level.
Das auf dem Niveau des Wohnraumes liegende Schwimmbecken
im Garten.

The summer house on the slope, containing a workshop and the caretaker's apartment.
Das am Hang liegende Gartenhaus mit Atelier und Hausmeisterwohnung.

View from the living room looking toward the swimming pool and garden.
Blick aus dem Wohnraum auf Schwimmbecken und Garten.

Pedregulho Residential Neighborhood, Rio de Janeiro – commenced 1947

Structural engineers:
Sydney Santos and David Astrachan

Some fifteen minutes away by car via the Avenida Brasil from the center of Rio de Janeiro lies Pedregulho Hill, on the western side of which this residential neighborhood was laid out for lower-paid municipal workers. At the First Biennale in São Paulo in 1951, Reidy's design was awarded the prize for the best plan for the organization of large areas.

The site, which covers some 12 acres, has differences in levels of as much as 164 ft. The main water reservoirs are situated nearby, as are many municipal services in which the tenants of the Pedregulho neighborhood are employed. Apart from the actual dwelling blocks, the scheme also includes such social installations as a school, playground, health center, shopping center, and laundry. The municipal housing office instituted careful inquiries into the economic and social circumstances of the future tenants. The results showed that various types of apartments would be required. The four blocks, of which three have so far been completed, contain a total of 508 apartments—ranging in size from one-room apartments with bathroom and kitchen to apartments with four bedrooms, a living room, bathroom, and kitchen.

Families are examined for contagious disease before moving in. The tenancy agreement contains a regulation allowing the apartments to be inspected from time to time by officials of the municipal workers' housing department. The rent is deducted from the wages and includes the washing of 4 lb. of laundry per person per week. Refuse is collected and burned.

All connecting streets between the various buildings are kept free from motor traffic. Inhabitants of block C reach the main area through a small tunnel which passes under the only road to cut across the site. Each block has approach roads from the periphery and parking facilities. The garden was designed by Roberto Burle-Marx.

The blocks of apartments are raised from the ground on pillars. This results in shaded areas underneath the buildings and good air circulation, which is particularly valuable during the summer months. Wherever the use of expensive sun-screen could be avoided, perforated ceramic units permitting the passage of light and air were used to afford protection against the sun.

Aerial view of the Pedregulho residential district.
Luftansicht des Pedregulho-Wohngebiets.

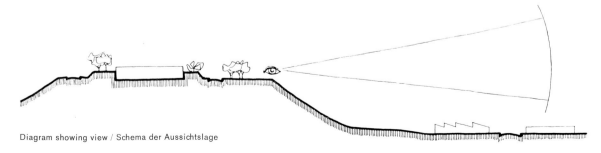

Diagram showing view / Schema der Aussichtslage

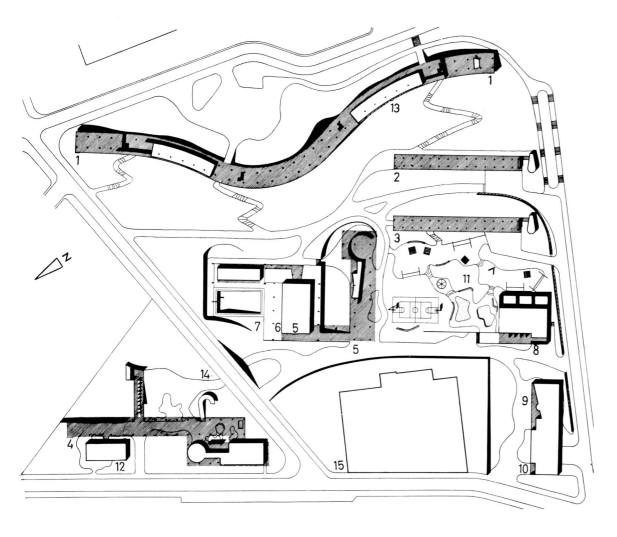

General site plan, scale 1:2,000 / Lageplan
1 Apartment block A / Wohnblock A
2 Apartment block B1 / Wohnblock B1
3 Apartment block B2 / Wohnblock B2
4 Apartment block C / Wohnblock C
5 Elementary school / Grundschule
6 Gymnasium / Turnhalle
7 Swimming pool / Schwimmbecken
8 Health center / Gesundheitszentrum
9 Laundry / Wäscherei
10 Shopping center / Ladenzentrum
11 Playground / Spielplatz
12 Day nursery / Kinderhort
13 Kindergarten
14 Pedestrian subway / Fußgängerunterführung
15 Existing workshops / Bestehende Werkstätten

Pedregulho - Wohngebiet, Rio de Janeiro begonnen 1947

Statik: Sydney Santos und David Astrachan

Vom Zentrum Rio de Janeiros aus erreicht man mit dem Wagen in etwa 15 Minuten über die »Avenida Brasil« den Pedregulho-Hügel, an dessen westlichem Abhang dieses Wohngebiet für städtische Angestellte mit kleinem Einkommen angelegt wurde. Auf der ersten Biennale in São Paulo, 1951, wurde Reidys Entwurf mit dem Preis für das beste Projekt zur Organisation großer Gebiete ausgezeichnet.

Das etwa 5 ha große Gelände weist Höhenunterschiede bis zu 50 m auf. In der Umgebung liegen die Hauptwasserreservoirs und zum großen Teil städtische Werkstattbetriebe, in denen die Bewohner des Pedregulho-Gebiets beschäftigt sind. Das Programm umfaßt außer Wohnbauten auch alle sozialen Einrichtungen, wie Schule, Spielplatz, Gesundheitszentrum, Ladenzentrum und Wäscherei. Das städtische Amt für Wohnungsbau hatte genaue Untersuchungen über die wirtschaftlichen und sozialen Verhältnisse der zukünftigen Mieter angestellt. Das Ergebnis zeigte, daß verschiedene Wohnungstypen benötigt wurden. Die vier Blocks von denen bisher drei fertiggestellt wurden, enthalten insgesamt 508 Wohnungen, deren Größen von der Einraumwohnung mit Bad und Küche bis zu Wohnungen mit vier Schlafräumen, Bad und Küche gestaffelt sind. Die Familien werden vor dem Einzug auf ansteckende Krankheiten untersucht. Der Mietvertrag enthält die obligatorische Bestimmung, daß die Wohnungen von Zeit zu Zeit von Beamten des städtischen Arbeitersiedlungswerks inspiziert werden. Die Miete wird vom Gehalt einbehalten und schließt die Reinigung von 2 kg Wäsche pro Person und Woche ein. Die Abfälle werden gesammelt und verbrannt.

Alle Verbindungswege zwischen den einzelnen Gebäuden sind von motorisiertem Verkehr freigehalten. Die Bewohner von Block C erreichen das Hauptgebiet durch einen kleinen Tunnel, der unter der einzigen das Gelände kreuzenden Straße hindurchführt. Jeder Block hat von der Peripherie her Zufahrten und Parkmöglichkeiten. Die Gartengestaltung lag in den Händen von Roberto Burle-Marx.

Die Wohnblocks sind durch Pilotis vom Terrain abgehoben; dadurch ergeben sich unter den Bauten schattige Freiflächen und zugleich entsteht eine ausgezeichnete Luftzirkulation, die sich besonders während der Sommermonate günstig auswirkt. Wo aufwendige Sonnenbrecher vermieden werden konnten, wurden Hohlziegel angewandt, die licht- und luftdurchlässig sind und vor der Sonne schützen.

Block A

Situated at the highest level, block A follows the line of the hill along its length of 853 ft. and contains 272 apartments of various kinds. On the side facing the hill, two bridges connect the street and the third floor from which three main flights of stairs afford access to the apartment floors. This solution eliminated the expense of installing elevators. With the exception of rooms for administration, social workers, day nursery, and kindergarten, the third floor is free from partition walls and is used in part as a playground for children. At the extreme end, there is a shell-shaped sound reflector for a children's theater. Below there are two floors with one-room apartments, and above there are two floors with duplex apartments containing from one to four bedrooms. The floor plan and the construction of the building were designed so that the supports pass through the adjoining walls of the apartments. Some of the space thus made available was utilized for built-in cupboards.

Block A

Der am höchsten gelegene Block A ist mit seinen 260 m Länge dem Verlauf des Hügels angepaßt und enthält 272 Wohnungen verschiedenen Typs. Auf der dem Hügel zugewandten Seite bilden zwei Brücken die Verbindung zwischen Straße und drittem Geschoß, von dem aus durch drei Haupttreppen die Wohngeschosse zu erreichen sind. Durch diese Lösung konnten hohe Kosten für Aufzüge vermieden werden. Das dritte Geschoß, das zum Teil als Kinderspielplatz dient, ist bis auf einige Räume für Verwaltung, Sozialhelfer, Kinderkrippe und Kindergarten frei von Trennwänden. Am äußersten Ende befindet sich eine Schallmuschel für ein Kindertheater. Darunter liegen zwei Geschosse mit Einraumwohnungen, darüber zwei Geschosse mit Duplexwohnungen, die ein bis vier Schlafräume enthalten. Grundriß und Konstruktion des Gebäudes wurden so miteinander in Übereinstimmung gebracht, daß die Stützen innerhalb der Wohnungstrennwände verlaufen. Die sich ergebenden Hohlräume wurden teilweise für eingebaute Schränke ausgenutzt.

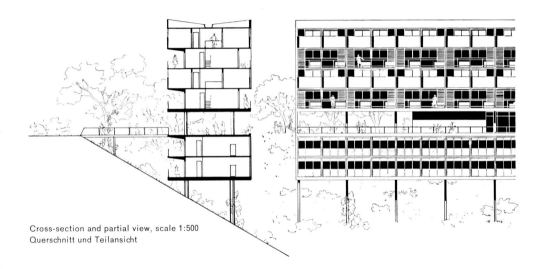

Cross-section and partial view, scale 1:500
Querschnitt und Teilansicht

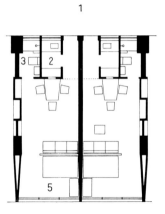

First- and second-floor plan, scale 1:200
Grundriß 1. und 2. Geschoß

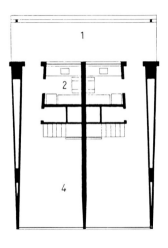

Fourth- and sixth-floor plan, scale 1:200
Grundriß 4. und 6. Geschoß

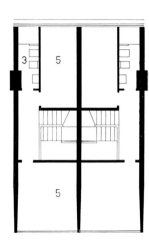

Fifth- and seventh-floor plan, scale 1:200
Grundriß 5. und 7. Geschoß

Captions to the floor plans for one-room and duplex apartments
Legende zu den Grundrissen der Einraum- und Duplexwohnungen
1 Corridor / Gang
2 Kitchen / Küche
3 Lavatory / Toilette
4 Living room / Wohnraum
5 Bedroom / Schlafraum
6 Bridge / Brücke
7 Administration, social welfare / Verwaltung, Sozialfürsorge
8 Nursery school / Spielschule
9 Children's theater / Kindertheater
10 Kindergarten
11 Incinerator for refuse / Abfallverbrennung
12 Water tank / Wasserbehälter
13 Expansion joint / Dehnungsfuge

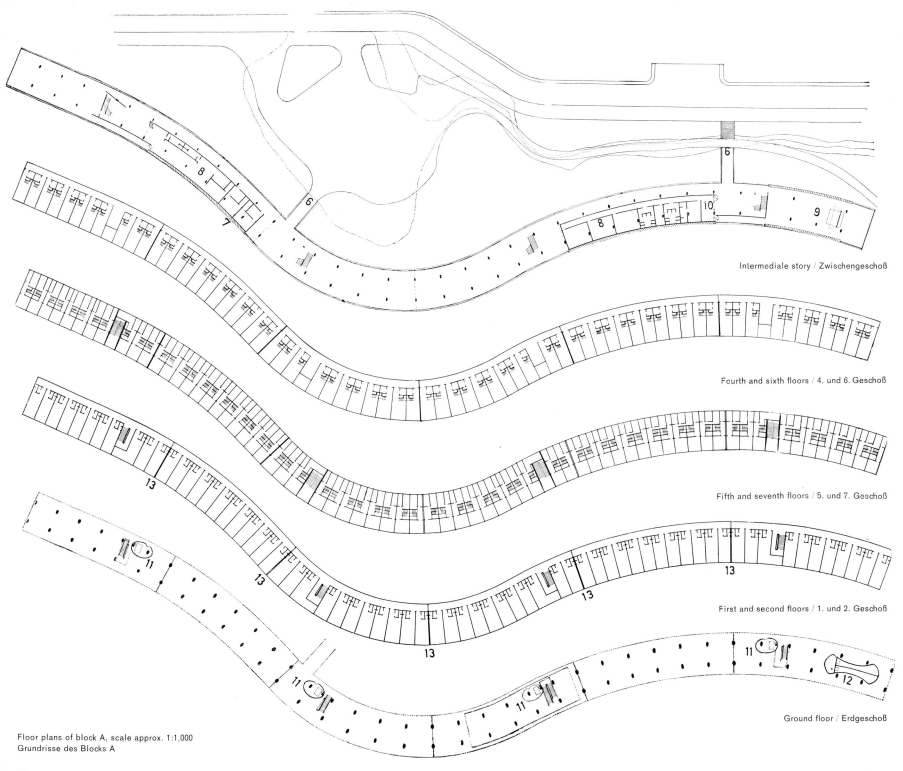

Intermediale story / Zwischengeschoß

Fourth and sixth floors / 4. und 6. Geschoß

Fifth and seventh floors / 5. und 7. Geschoß

First and second floors / 1. und 2. Geschoß

Ground floor / Erdgeschoß

Floor plans of block A, scale approx. 1:1,000
Grundrisse des Blocks A

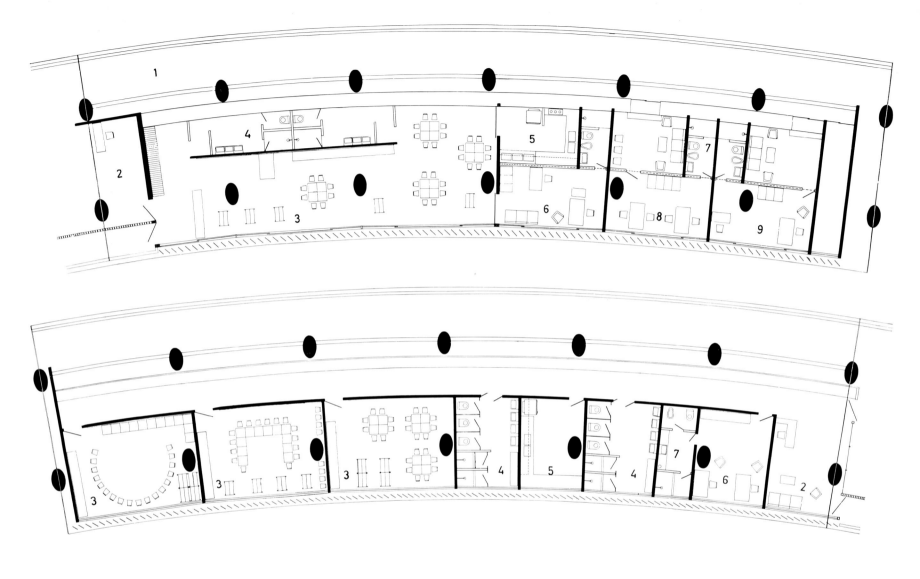

Sections from the intermediate story (nursery school, social welfare,
administration), scale 1:200
Ausschnitte aus dem Zwischengeschoß (Spielschule, Sozialfürsorge.
Verwaltung)
1 Corridor / Gang
2 Inquiries / Anmeldung
3 Playroom / Spielzimmer
4 Lavatories (children) / Toiletten (Kinder)
5 Kitchen / Küche
6 Teacher's room / Lehrerzimmer
7 Lavatory / Toilette
8 Social welfare / Sozialfürsorge
9 House administrator / Hausverwalter

View of block A. On the left, the school; on the right, the health
center, behind block B.
Ansicht von Block A. Links Schule, rechts Gesundheitszentrum,
dahinter Block B.

Page / Seite 102 + 103
View of the curved block A, looking from the intermediate story.
Der gekurvte Block A vom Zwischengeschoß aus.

Blocks B1 and B2

The four-story blocks B1 and B2 are approximately 262 ft. long, and each contains two rows with a total of 112 duplex apartments which are divided into types with two, three, and four bedrooms. These two blocks were first occupied in 1950. Block C, which is not yet completed, is designed as a twelve-story block of apartments and will be the only one in the group to have elevators.

Block B1 und B2

Die viergeschossigen Blocks B1 und B2 sind annähernd 80 m lang und enthalten je zwei Reihen mit insgesamt 112 Duplexwohnungen, die in Typen mit zwei, drei und vier Schlafräumen aufgeteilt sind. Diese beiden Blocks wurden 1950 bezogen. Der noch nicht fertiggestellte Block C ist als 12-geschossiges Wohnhaus geplant, das als einziges dieser Gruppe mit Aufzügen versehen wird.

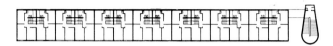

Second- and fourth-floor plan, scale 1:1,000
Grundriß 2. und 4. Geschoß

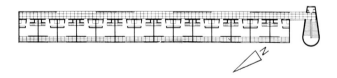

First- and third-floor plan, scale 1:1,000
Grundriß 1. und 3. Geschoß

Ground-floor plan, scale 1:1,000 / Grundriß Erdgeschoß

Captions to plan of various kinds of duplex apartments
Legende zu den Grundrissen der Duplexwohnungen verschiedenen Typs
1 Corridor / Gang
2 Kitchen / Küche
3 Living room / Wohnraum
4 Loggia
5 Bedroom / Schlafraum
6 Bath / Bad

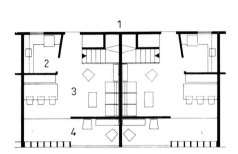

Duplex apartment: lower floor, scale 1:200
Duplexwohnung, unteres Geschoß

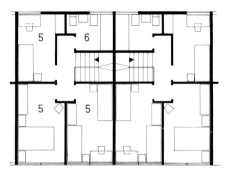

Duplex apartment: upper floor, scale 1:200
Duplexwohnung, oberes Geschoß

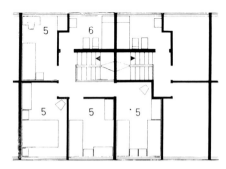

Duplex apartment: alternate design
for upper floor, scale 1:200
Duplexwohnung, oberes Geschoß. Variante

104

Block B1: general view / Block B1: Gesamtansicht

Block B: section of the façade on the northwest side.
Block B: Fassadenausschnitt der Nordwestseite.

View of interior of a living room in Block B.
Innenansicht eines Wohnraums in Block B.

Block B: section of façade, with separate stairwell.
Block B: Fassadenausschnitt mit dem freistehenden Treppenturm.

View of interior of a duplex apartment in block B. On the right, the staircase to the upper floor.
Innenansicht einer Duplexwohnung im Block B. Rechts die Treppe zum oberen Geschoß.

Primary School

The low school building is intended for 200 children from age seven to eleven. Five classrooms accommodating forty pupils each are arranged on the southern side of the main building, which is supported by pillars. Access is gained by means of a covered ramp and a corridor on the north side. On the ground floor, the free space between the pillars is used as a covered playground. Lavatories, a kitchen, and a room for light refreshments are also located here. The layout is completed in the northeast by a gymnasium and a swimming pool measuring 39 x 82 ft.

Grundschule

Das niedrige Schulgebäude ist für 200 Kinder im Alter von 7 bis 11 Jahren bestimmt. Fünf Klassenräume für je 40 Schüler liegen auf der Südseite des von Pilotis getragenen Hauptgeschosses. Der Zugang erfolgt über eine gedeckte Rampe und einen Gang auf der Nordseite. Im Erdgeschoß wird der freie Raum zwischen den Pilotis als gedeckter Spielplatz benutzt. Außerdem befinden sich dort Toiletten, eine Küche und ein Imbißraum. Im Nordosten wird die Anlage durch eine Turnhalle und ein 12 x 25 m großes Schwimmbecken vervollständigt.

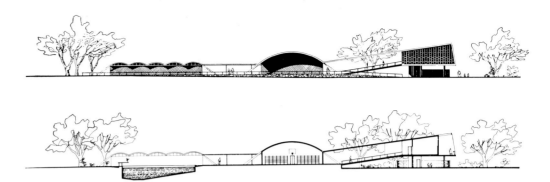

View and longitudinal section, scale 1:1,000
Ansicht und Längsschnitt

Top-floor plan, scale 1:1,000 / Grundriß Obergeschoß

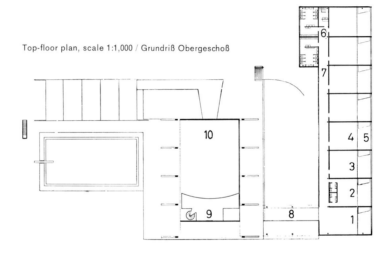

Ground-floor plan, scale 1:1,000 / Grundriß Erdgeschoß

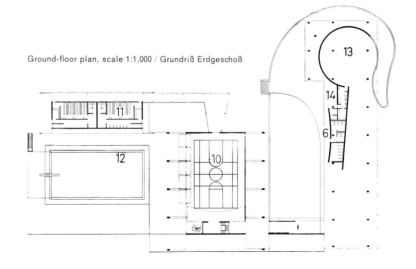

Captions to plans / Legende zu den Grundrissen
 1 Entrance hall and administration / Vorhalle und Verwaltung
 2 Secretariat and school management / Sekretariat und Schulleitung
 3 Library / Bibliothek
 4 Classrooms / Klassenräume
 5 Terrace / Terrasse
 6 Lavatories / Toiletten
 7 Corridor / Gang
 8 Ramp / Rampe
 9 Balcony / Galerie
10 Gymnasium / Turnhalle
11 Dressing rooms / Umkleideräume
12 Swimming pool / Schwimmbecken
13 Snack room / Imbißraum
14 Kitchen / Küche

Gymnasium (left) and school building. Ceramic wall from a design
by Candido Portinari.
Turnhalle (links) und Schulgebäude. Wand aus Keramikplatten nach
einem Entwurf von Candido Portinari.

Window on the corridor along the north side of the classroom story: open concrete frame set in grill.
Fenster am Gang auf der Nordseite des Klassengeschosses: offener Betonrahmen zwischen Hohlsteinen.

The covered approach ramp to the classroom story. ▷
Die überdachte Zugangsrampe zum Klassengeschoß.

110

The classroom block looking from the west. The open, shaded space beneath the pillars on the ground floor serves as a playground.
Der Klassentrakt von Westen. Der freie, schattige Raum zwischen den Pilotis im Erdgeschoß dient als Spielplatz.

Mosaic wall from a design by Roberto Burle-Marx.
Mosaikwand nach einem Entwurf von Roberto Burle-Marx.

Corridor connecting to the classrooms on the main floor.
Verbindungsgang zu den Klassenräumen im Hauptgeschoß.

View looking into a classroom.
Blick in einen Klassenraum.

Approach to the gallery of the gymnasium.
Zugang zum Galeriegeschoß der Turnhalle.

View from the gymnasium looking toward the swimming pool and the dressing rooms.
Blick aus der Turnhalle auf Schwimmbecken und Umkleideräume.

The wing with the dressing rooms and the swimming pool. ▷
Der Flügel mit den Umkleideräumen und Schwimmbecken.

Shopping center and laundry

The shopping center and laundry are accommodated by the side of a road on the margin of the site. The arrangement of separate entrances for suppliers and parking space for the loading and unloading of trucks eliminates any inconvenience to the public. An opening along the full length of the roof ensures cross-ventilation. The selling space is protected from the sun on the north side by movable, horizontal sun-screens. The building is equipped with cold-storage rooms and showcases, an electric oven, and electric washing and ironing machines.

Ladenzentrum und Wäscherei

An einer Verkehrsstraße am Rande der Gesamtanlage sind in einem eingeschossigen Gebäude Ladenzentrum und Wäscherei untergebracht. Durch gesonderte Lieferanteneingänge und Parkgelegenheiten zum Be- und Entladen von Lastwagen wird eine Behinderung des Publikums vermieden. Ein Dacheinschnitt über die ganze Länge des Gebäudes sorgt für Querlüftung. Der Verkaufsraum wird auf der Nordseite durch bewegliche horizontale Sonnenblenden geschützt. Die Anlage ist mit Kühlräumen, Kühltheken, einem elektrischen Backofen und elektrischen Wasch- und Bügelmaschinen ausgestattet.

Cross-section, scale 1:500 / Querschnitt

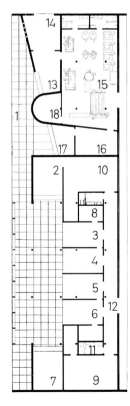

Floor plan, scale 1:500 / Grundriß

Captions to floor plan / Legende zum Grundriß
1 Customers' entrance / Kundeneingang
2 Groceries / Kolonialwaren
3 Butcher shop / Fleischerei
4 Fish / Fischwaren
5 Fruit and vegetables / Obst und Gemüse
6 Dairy products / Milchprodukte
7 Baker's shop / Backwaren
8 Cold storage / Kühlraum
9 Bakery / Bäckerei
10 Storeroom / Lagerraum
11 Lavatory / Toilette
12 Suppliers' entrance / Lieferanteneingang
13 Laundry intake / Wäscheannahme
14 Water heater / Boiler
15 Laundry / Wäscherei
16 Finished laundry / Fertige Wäsche
17 Laundry delivery / Wäscheausgabe
18 Administration / Verwaltung

General view of the shopping center, with the horizontal sun blinds
on the northern side.
Gesamtansicht des Ladenzentrums mit den horizontalen Sonnenblenden der Nordseite.

Health center

The health center—which is intended for medical treatment, dental treatment, preventive measures, first aid, and minor operations—is accommodated in another one-story building. The rooms, which face south, open into pergola-like sections of garden.

Gesundheitszentrum

In einem weiteren eingeschossigen Bau befindet sich das Gesundheitszentrum, das für ärztliche Behandlung, Zahnbehandlung, vorbeugende Maßnahmen, erste Hilfe und kleinere Operationen gedacht ist. Die nach Südosten gelegenen Räume öffnen sich auf pergola-artige Gartenabschnitte.

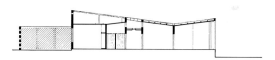

Cross-section, scale 1:500 / Querschnitt

Ground plan, scale 1:500 / Grundriß

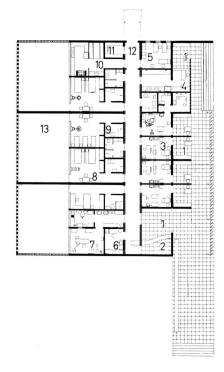

Captions to the floor plan / Legende zum Grundriß
1 Vestibule / Vorraum
2 Inquiries / Anmeldung
3 Treatment rooms / Behandlungsräume
4 Pharmacy / Apotheke
5 Administration / Verwaltung
6 Laboratories / Laboratorien
7 Operating theater / Operationsraum
8 Sick ward / Krankenzimmer
9 Lavatories / Toiletten
10 Dining room and kitchen / Eßraum und Küche
11 Laundry / Wäsche
12 Staff entrance / Personaleingang
13 Garden / Garten

The entrance side of the health center. Ceramic wall from a design
by Anisio Medeiros.
Eingangsseite des Gesundheitszentrums. Wand aus Keramikplatten
nach einem Entwurf von Anisio Medeiros.

Gávea Residential Neighborhood, Rio de Janeiro
commenced 1952

Structural engineers: Sydney Santos, David Astrachan, Carlos de Oliveira Góes

This residential neighborhood took shape south of the town on a site with a total area of 35 acres at a height of up to 217 ft. above sea level, surrounded by mountains. In its general site plan, the project is similar to the Pedregulho residential neighborhood. Apart from the residential blocks, it contains such important social installations as an elementary school, day nursery, kindergarten, playgrounds, health center, laundry, and shopping center. Thoroughfares for pedestrians and motor vehicles are separate.

A total of 748 apartments is accommodated in block A, which is curvilinear in shape to fit the terrain, and in seven blocks of type B. The density of the population is 300 inhabitants per hectare (2.47 acres). The elevated position affords a view of the mountains and the lagoon. Formerly, more than 5,000 persons lived here in wooden huts under the most primitive conditions.

Wohngebiet Gávea, Rio de Janeiro – begonnen 1952

Statiker: Sydney Santos, David Astrachan, Carlos de Oliveira Góes

Dieses Wohngebiet entsteht südlich der Stadt auf einem 114000 qm großen Gelände, das bis zu 66 m über dem Meeresspiegel liegt und von Bergen umgeben ist. Das Projekt ähnelt in seiner Gesamtanlage dem Pedregulho-Wohngebiet. Es umfaßt außer den Wohnbauten alle wichtigen sozialen Einrichtungen wie Grundschule, Kinderkrippe, Kindergarten, Spielplätze, Gesundheitszentrum, Wäscherei und Einkaufszentrum. Die Verkehrswege für Fußgänger und Fahrzeuge liegen getrennt.

Insgesamt 748 Wohnungen verteilen sich auf den in seiner Biegung dem Gelände angepaßten Block A und auf sieben Blocks vom Typ B. Die Wohndichte beträgt 300 Einwohner pro Hektar. Durch die erhöhte Lage ergibt sich eine Aussicht auf das Gebirge und die Lagune. Bisher wohnten hier über 5000 Personen unter primitivsten Bedingungen in Bretterhütten.

View of a model from the northwest (photomontage). In front, the seven blocks of type B; in the background, the curved block A.
Modellansicht von Nordwesten (Photomontage). Vorn die 7 Blocks vom Typ B, im Hintergrund der geschwungene Block A.

The Gávea residential neighborhood looking from one of the mountains in the west. In the center can be seen block A under construction.
Das Wohngebiet Gávea von einem der im Westen gelegenen Berge. Im Zentrum Block A im Bau.

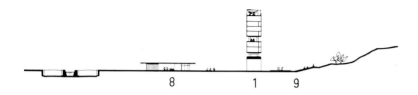

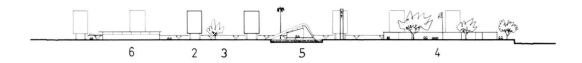

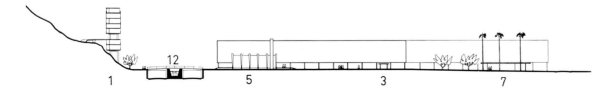

Transverse and longitudinal sections to general site plan, scale 1:2,000
Quer- und Längsschnitte zum Lageplan

Captions to site plan and sections
Legende zu Lageplan und Schnitten
1 Apartment block A / Wohnblock A
2 Apartment block B / Wohnblock B
3 Covered passage / Überdeckter Weg
4 Elementary school / Grundschule
5 Chapel / Kapelle
6 Health center / Gesundheitszentrum
7 Shopping center and laundry / Einkaufszentrum und Wäscherei
8 Kindergarten
9 Open-air theater / Freilichttheater
10 Bridge / Brücke
11 Children's playground / Kinderspielplatz
12 Pedestrian crossing / Fußgängerüberführung
13 Pool / Bassin
14 Parking area / Parkplatz
15 Footpath / Fußweg
16 Water reservoir / Wasserreservoir
17 Sports ground / Sportplatz

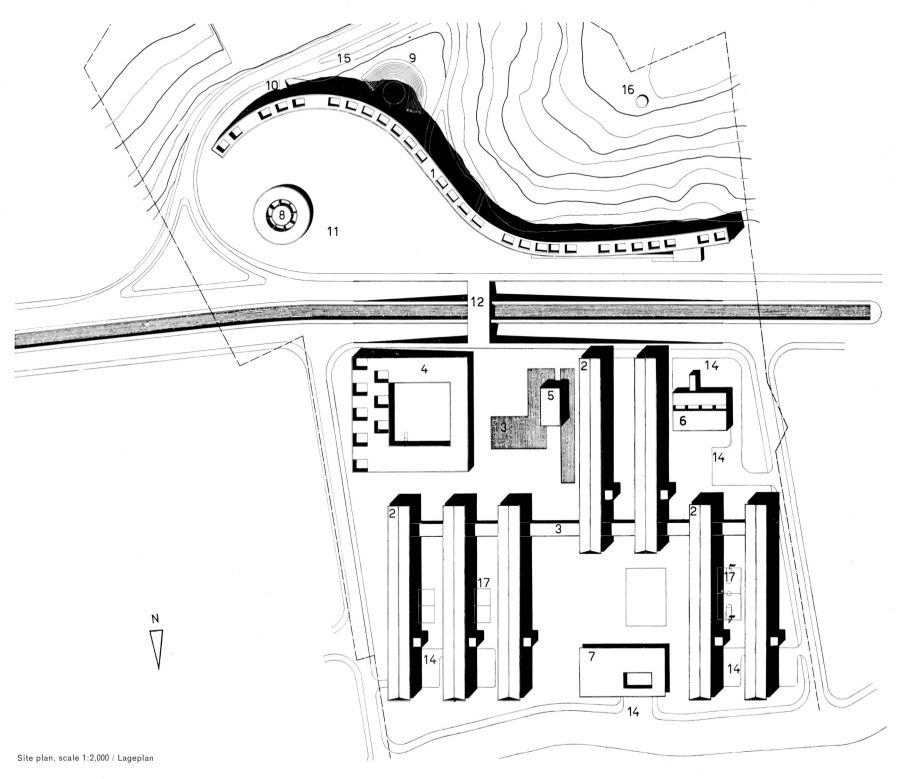

N

Site plan, scale 1:2,000 / Lageplan

121

Some of the huts which formerly occupied part of the site.
Einige der Bretterhütten, die früher einen Teil des Gebietes
einnahmen.

View from the north to block A during construction.
Ansicht von Norden auf Block A im Rohbau.

Block A

As in the Pedregulho project, access to block A is by way of a concourse floor reached from the slope. Below are two stories with one-room apartments and a separate bed alcove, and above there are four floors with duplex apartments entered from an arcade. Various communal installations are accommodated on the top floor.

Block A

Ähnlich wie beim Pedregulho-Projekt wird der Block A vom Hang aus durch ein Verteilergeschoß erschlossen. Darunter liegen zwei Geschosse mit Einraumwohnungen und abgetrennter Schlafkoje, darüber vier Geschosse mit Duplexwohnungen aus drei Wohnräumen, Küche und Bad. Die Wohnungen werden von Laubengängen aus betreten. Das Dachgeschoß nimmt verschiedene Gemeinschaftseinrichtungen auf.

First- and second-floor plan, scale 1:100
Grundriß 1. und 2. Obergeschoß

Fourth- and sixth-floor plan, scale 1:100
Grundriß 4. und 6. Obergeschoß

Fifth- and seventh-floor plan, scale 1:100
Grundriß 5. und 7. Obergeschoß

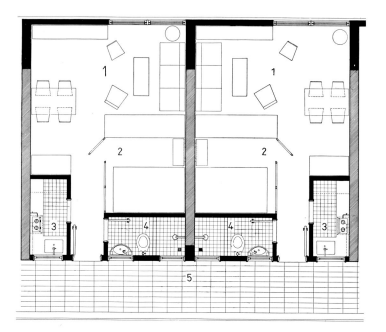
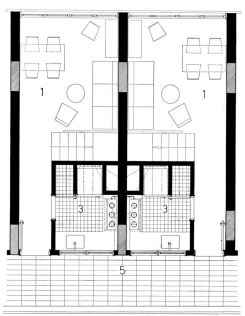
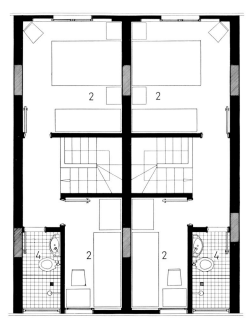

North façade (section, scale 1:500) / Nordfassade (Ausschnitt)

Section of the north front of block A during construction.
Ausschnitt aus der Nordfassade von Block A im Rohbau.

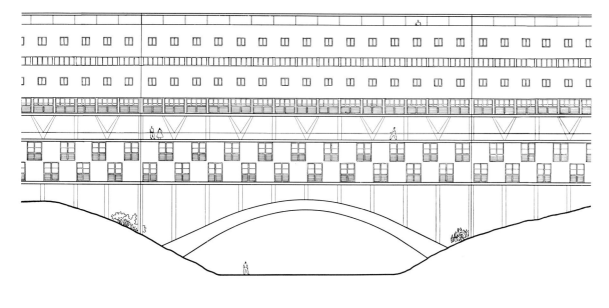

Captions to the plans / Legende zu den Grundrissen
1 Living room / Wohnraum
2 Bedroom / Schlafraum
3 Kitchen / Küche
4 Bathroom / Bad
5 Corridor / Gang

125

Block B

In the seven blocks of type B, duplex apartments comprising three or four living rooms are combined with two-room apartments arranged parallel and along the shaded south façade. Access to the individual apartments is by internal corridors on every second floor.

Block B

Bei den sieben Blocks vom Typ B sind Duplexwohnungen aus drei oder vier Wohnräumen mit parallel zur sonnenfreien Südfassade liegenden Zweiraumwohnungen kombiniert. Die einzelnen Wohnungen werden durch innenliegende Korridore in jedem zweiten Geschoß erschlossen.

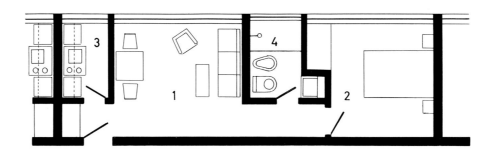

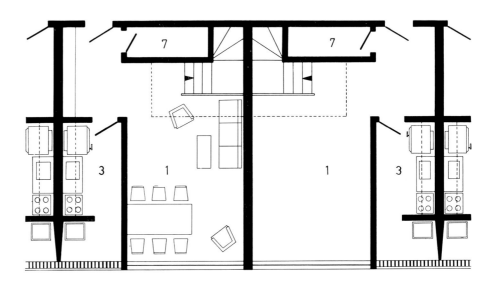

Floor plan of a lower-story unit, scale 1:100
Grundriß einer unteren Geschoßeinheit

Diagram showing how a lower floor is subdivided
Schema der Aufteilung innerhalb eines unteren Geschosses

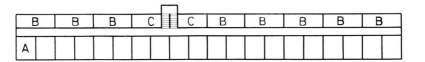

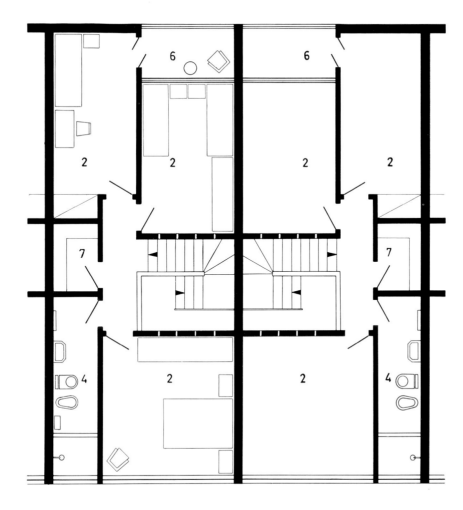

Captions to the plans / Legende zu den Grundrissen
1 Living room / Wohnraum
2 Bedroom / Schlafraum
3 Kitchen / Küche
4 Bath / Bad
5 Corridor / Gang
6 Loggia
7 Walk-in closet / Begehbarer Schrank

Floor plan of an upper-story unit, scale 1:100
Grundriß einer oberen Geschoßeinheit

Diagram showing how an upper floor is subdivided
Schema der Aufteilung innerhalb eines oberen Geschosses

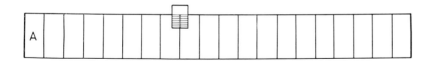

Aviation Training Center São José dos Campos, São Paulo – 1947

This design was submitted as an entry in a competition for an engineer training center for the aircraft industry and the Brazilian Air Force. It was awarded the third prize.

Apart from training, an important function of the center is to carry out research and experiments in the field of aviation. The whole project comprises a group of schools, laboratories, and research installations—as well as apartments and communal facilities, some of which are also intended to serve the existing town. The number of persons to be accommodated initially would be 4,000, of which 1,500 would be students and 2,500 instructors, employees, and their families. The area is divided into various zones in which thoroughfares for pedestrians and vehicles are entirely separate.

The residential area comprises apartment blocks, detached houses, and communal installations. These buildings include various arrangements of stories to suit teachers, assistants, and employees; accommodation for pupils of the preliminary and training schools, thirty-two detached houses for directors and teachers, an elementary school, and a restaurant. The inhabitants are within easy walking distance of their place of work. Administration, the preliminary school, and the training school are grouped in the school zone. The administration building lies between the two schools in the center of the layout. Double wings are provided for the schools, the uniform orientation of the classrooms being maintained by the use of double sawtooth roofs. The double wings have the advantage of cutting down distances and the amount of space allocated to circulation. The zone for maintenance and services contains the laundry, storehouse, workshops, garages, and a fireproof depot. These buildings are separated from the center and are connected to a military airfield by means of a bypass.

A group of laboratories and wind tunnels is located between the center and the civil airfield, at a sufficient distance from the school buildings.

On the opposite side, there are buildings for recreation, entertainment, and sports. This zone includes a gymnasium, a swimming pool, sports grounds, and an artificial boating lake. In front of the dam, which together with the contours of the terrain forms the confines of the lake, there is a stadium for 10,000 persons. There is also a building for cinema and theater performances, with seating accommodation for 2,000. A hospital is located a short distance away.

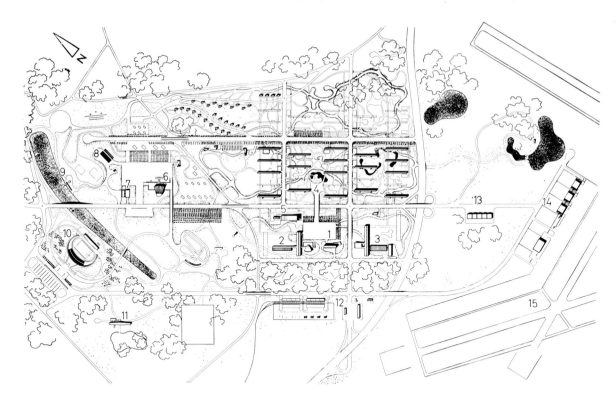

Site plan / Lageplan

Captions to site plan / Legende zum Lageplan
1 Administration / Verwaltung
2 Preliminary school / Vorschule
3 Training school / Ausbildungsschule
4 Residential buildings / Wohnbauten
5 Restaurant and shopping center / Restaurant und Einkaufszentrum
6 Theater
7 Gymnasium / Turnhalle
8 Swimming pool / Schwimmbecken
9 Lake / See
10 Stadium / Stadion
11 Hospital / Krankenhaus
12 Service zone / Versorgungszone
13 Laboratories / Laboratorien
14 Hangars
15 Civil airfield / Zivilflugplatz

Captions to the plans of the administration building
Legende zu den Grundrissen des Verwaltungsgebäudes
1 Canteen / Kantine
2 Bar
3 Entrance hall / Eingangshalle
4 Reception / Empfang
5 Post
6 Administration / Verwaltung
7 Lavatories / Toiletten
8 Hall and inquiry stand / Halle und Informationsstand
9 Offices and conference rooms
   Büro- und Besprechungsräume
10 Management rooms / Direktionsräume
11 Conference rooms / Besprechungsräume
12 Management rooms / Direktionsräume
13 Photographic department / Fotoabteilung

Southwest view of the administration building, scale 1:1,000
Südwestansicht des Verwaltungsgebäudes

Northeast view of the administration building, scale 1:1,000
Nordostansicht des Verwaltungsgebäudes

Cross and longitudinal section, scale 1:1,000 / Quer- und Längsschnitt

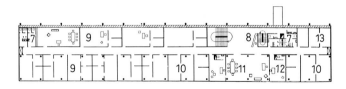

First upper-floor plan, scale 1:1,000 / Grundriß 1. Obergeschoß

Ground-floor plan, scale 1:1,000 / Grundriß Erdgeschoß

Basement plan, scale 1:1,000
Grundriß Kellergeschoß

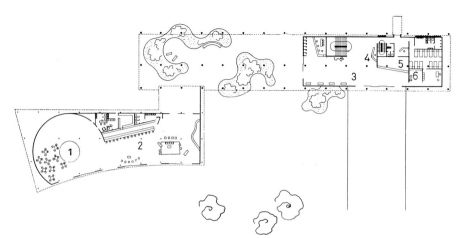

Luftfahrtausbildungszentrum São José dos Campos, São Paulo – 1947

Dieses Projekt entstand in einem Wettbewerb für ein Zentrum zur Ausbildung von Technikern der Luftfahrtindustrie und der brasilianischen Luftwaffe. Es wurde mit dem dritten Preis ausgezeichnet.

Neben der Schulung ist ein wesentliches Ziel dieses Zentrums, Forschungen und Experimente auf dem Gebiet der Luftfahrt durchzuführen. Die Gesamtanlage besteht aus einer Gruppe von Schulen, Laboratorien und Forschungsstätten, ferner Wohnungen und Gemeinschaftseinrichtungen, von denen einige auch der schon bestehenden Stadt dienen sollen. Die Zahl der unterzubringenden Personen wurde zunächst mit 4000 angegeben, davon 1500 Studenten und 2500 Lehrer, Angestellte und deren Familien. Das Gebiet umfaßt verschiedene Zonen mit völlig getrennten Verkehrswegen für Fußgänger und Fahrzeuge.

Die Wohnzone besteht aus Apartmenthäusern, Einzelhäusern und Gemeinschaftseinrichtungen. Diese Gebäude enthalten verschiedene Geschoßtypen für Lehrer, Assistenten und Angestellte und Unterkünfte für die Schüler der Vor- und Ausbildungsschule, 32 Einzelhäuser für Direktoren und Lehrer, eine Grundschule und ein Restaurant. Die Einwohner können zu Fuß bequem ihre Arbeitsplätze erreichen.

In der Schulzone sind Verwaltung, Vorschule und Ausbildungsschule zusammengefaßt. Das Verwaltungsgebäude liegt zwischen den beiden Schulen im Zentrum der Anlage. Für die Schulen wurden Doppelflügel vorgesehen, in denen durch Doppelsheds die einheitliche Orientierung der Klassenräume gewahrt bleibt. Der Vorteil der Doppelflügel liegt in der Reduktion der Entfernungen und der Verkehrsflächen.

Die Zone für Unterhalt und Versorgung enthält Wäscherei, Lagerhaus, Werkstätten, Garagen und ein feuersicheres Depot. Diese Gebäude liegen vom Zentrum getrennt und sind durch eine Umgehungsstraße mit einem Militärflugplatz verbunden.

Zwischen dem Zentrum und dem Zivilflugplatz liegt in genügender Entfernung von den Schulgebäuden eine Gruppe von Laboratorien und Windkanälen.

Auf der gegenüber liegenden Seite befinden sich Bauten für Erholung, Unterhaltung und Sport. Diese Zone umfaßt Turnhalle, Schwimmbecken, Sportplätze und einen künstlichen Rudersee. Vor dem Damm, der unter Ausnutzung der topographischen Gegebenheiten den See begrenzt, befindet sich ein Stadion für 10000 Personen. Ferner ist hier ein Gebäude für Film- und Theateraufführungen vorgesehen, das 2000 Personen faßt. Etwas weiter abseits liegt ein Krankenhaus.

Preliminary school: view, scale 1:1,000 / Vorschule. Ansicht

Preliminary school: longitudinal section, scale 1:1,000
Vorschule. Längsschnitt

Preliminary school: ground-floor plan, scale 1:1,000
Vorschule. Grundriß Erdgeschoß

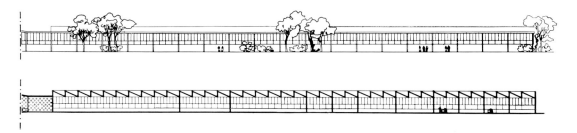

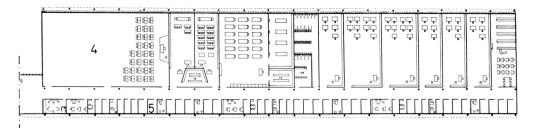

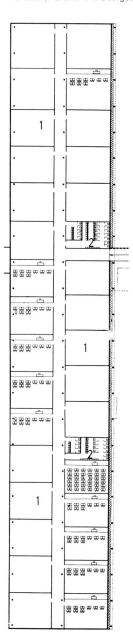

Captions to the plans of the preliminary school
Legende zu den Grundrissen der Vorschule
1 Classrooms / Klassenräume
2 Lavatories / Toiletten
3 Auditorium
4 Classrooms (practical) / Klassenräume (Übungen)
5 Teachers and assistants / Lehrer und Assistenten

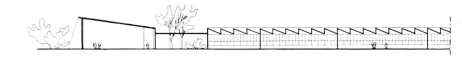

Training school: section, scale 1:1,000
Ausbildungsschule. Schnitt

Training school: partial section, scale 1:1,000
Ausbildungsschule. Teilschnitt

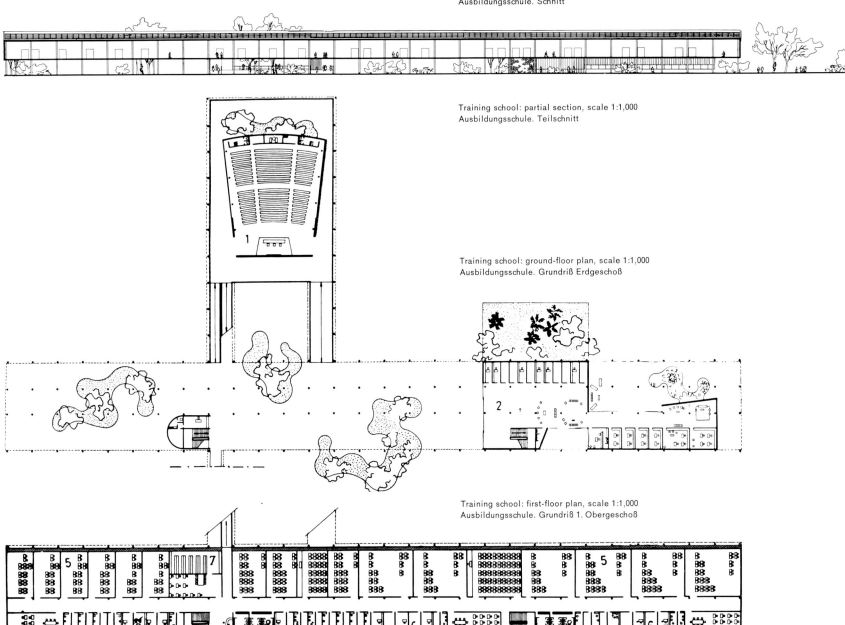

Training school: ground-floor plan, scale 1:1,000
Ausbildungsschule. Grundriß Erdgeschoß

Training school: first-floor plan, scale 1:1,000
Ausbildungsschule. Grundriß 1. Obergeschoß

Training school: partial view, scale 1:1,000
Ausbildungsschule. Teilansicht

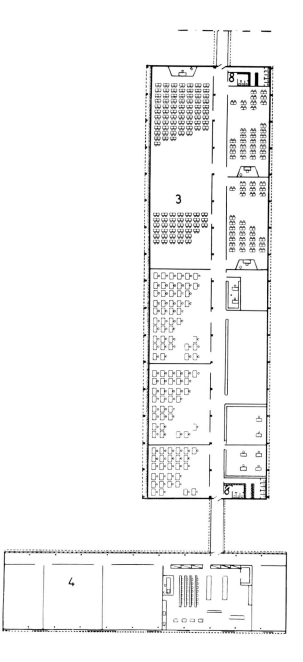

Ground-floor plan (annex), scale 1:1,000
Grundriß Erdgeschoß (Anschluß)

Captions to the floor plans of the training school
Legende zu den Grundrissen der Ausbildungsschule
1 Auditorium
2 Administration / Verwaltung
3 Classrooms (practical) / Klassenräume (Übungen)
4 Laboratories / Laboratorien
5 Classrooms (theoretical) / Klassenräume (Theorie)
6 Teachers and assistants / Lehrer und Assistenten
7 Library / Bibliothek

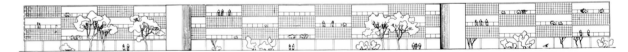

Students' home: northeast view, scale 1:1,000
Studentenheim. Nordostansicht

Students' home: southwest view, scale 1:1,000
Studentenheim. Südwestansicht

Students' home: longitudinal section, scale 1:1,000
Studentenheim. Längsschnitt

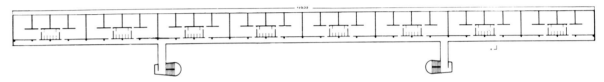

Students' home: standard upper-floor plan, scale 1:1,000
Studentenheim. Typen-Grundriß der Obergeschosse

Students' home: ground-floor plan, scale 1:1,000
Studentenheim. Grundriß des Erdgeschosses

Section of floor containing living quarters, scale 1:200
Wohngeschoßausschnitt

Cross-section, scale 1:200 / Querschnitt

Captions to the plans of the students' home
Legende zu den Grundrissen des Studentenheims
1 Dormitory / Schlafraum
2 Workroom / Arbeitsraum
3 Dressing room / Ankleideraum
4 Showers, lavatories, hand basins
  Duschen, Toiletten, Waschbecken

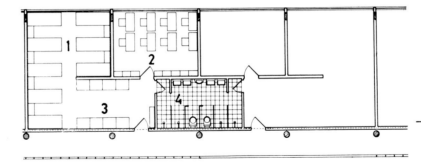

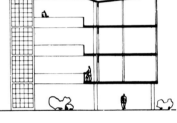

Restaurant and shopping center: northeast view, scale 1:1,000
Restaurant und Einkaufszentrum. Nordostansicht

Restaurant and shopping center: southwest view, scale 1:1,000
Restaurant und Einkaufszentrum. Südwestansicht

Longitudinal section, scale 1:1000 / Längsschnitt

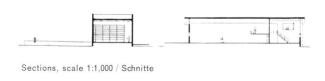

Sections, scale 1:1,000 / Schnitte

Restaurant and shopping center: floor plan,
scale 1:1,000
Restaurant und Einkaufszentrum. Grundriß

Captions to plan of restaurant and shopping center
Legende zum Grundriß von Restaurant und Einkaufszentrum
1 Restaurant
2 Kitchen / Küche
3 Lavatories / Toiletten
4 Bakery / Bäckerei
5 Covered platform / Überdeckte Plattform
6 Administration / Verwaltung
7 Shopping center / Einkaufszentrum

Plan for a new city center, Rio de Janeiro – 1948

This area is intended to form the new city center and is one of the new town-planning projects of Rio de Janeiro upon which work has already started. The removal of the Santo Antonio hill and the clearing of the whole area will make available a site of 73 acres for municipal buildings and business and residential blocks. The two-level north-south road will form a connection between the Avenida Presidente Vargas and the coast roads which will pass by way of tunnels to the residential areas farther south. These roads will also be widened by building up a coastal strip of sand.

Three historically valuable buildings dating from colonial times will be preserved: a monastery, a church, and an aqueduct which has been used for many years as a streetcar viaduct. Parallel to the north-south road, the plan is divided into three strips: on one side of the road, there is the municipal center with a thirty-story town hall, a museum designed by Le Corbusier, a library, an exhibition building, and a congress hall; on the other side lies the business center consisting of four 26-story buildings with shops and offices, a cinema, a theater, restaurants, and cafés; behind, there are twelve-story blocks of flats for some 8,000 persons, with a total living space of 49 acres, together with social services such as education, recreation, sports, and health which are required for this residential district.

Plan für ein neues Stadtzentrum, Rio de Janeiro – 1948

Als eines der bereits in Angriff genommenen Projekte der städtebaulichen Neuplanung Rio de Janeiros wird dieses Gebiet das künftige Stadtzentrum bilden. Durch Abtragen des Santo Antonio-Hügels und Sanieren des gesamten Gebietes entsteht ein 297 000 qm großes Gelände, das städtische Einrichtungen, Geschäfts- und Wohnbauten aufnehmen soll. Die zweigeschossige Nord-Süd-Straße stellt die Verbindung zwischen der Avenida Presidente Vargas und den Küstenstraßen her, die durch Tunnels in die weiter südlich gelegenen Wohngebiete führen und durch einen aufgeschütteten Strandstreifen verbreitert werden.

Drei historisch wertvolle Bauten aus der Kolonialzeit bleiben erhalten: ein Kloster, eine Kirche und ein Aquädukt, der jahrelang als Straßenbahnüberführung benutzt wurde. Parallel zur Nord-Süd-Straße gliedert sich die Planung in drei Streifen: auf der einen Seite das städtische Zentrum mit einem 30-geschossigen Rathaus, einem von Le Corbusier entworfenen Museum, einer Bibliothek, einem Ausstellungsgebäude und einer Kongreßhalle; auf der anderen Straßenseite das Ge-

schäftszentrum: vier 26-geschossige Gebäude mit Läden und Büros, ein Kino, ein Theater, Restaurants und Cafés; dahinter 12-geschossige Wohnhäuser für etwa 8000 Menschen mit einer Gesamtwohnfläche von 200 000 qm, ferner die für dieses Wohnviertel notwendigen sozialen Einrichtungen für Erziehung, Erholung, Sport und Gesundheit.

General plan / Übersichtsplan
1 Center / Zentrum
2 North-south road / Nord-Süd-Straße
3 Avenida Presidente Vargas
4 Coastal strip to be filled in and raised
  Aufzuschüttender Küstenstreifen

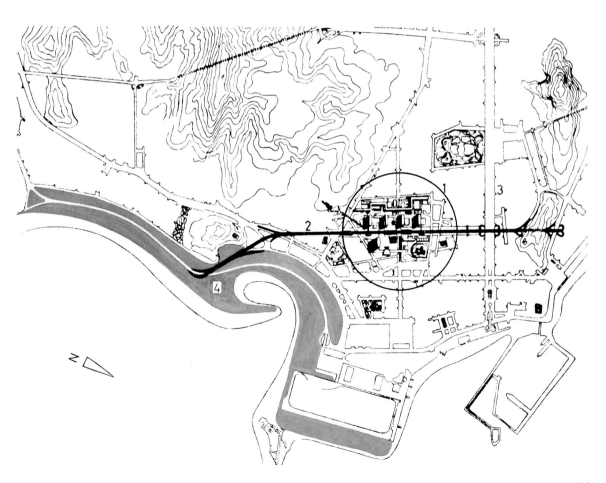

The aqueduct served for a long time as a streetcar connection
between two hills.
Der Aquädukt diente lange Zeit als Straßenbahnverbindung
zwischen zwei Hügeln.

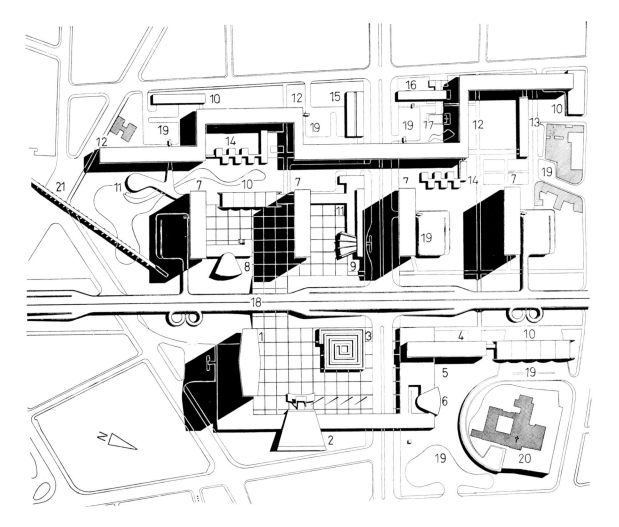

Site plan, scale 1:5,000 / Lageplan
Municipal buildings / Städtische Einrichtungen
 1 Town hall / Rathaus
 2 Municipal administration / Stadtverwaltung
 3 Municipal museum / Städtisches Museum
 4 Municipal library / Stadtbibliothek
 5 Exhibition hall / Ausstellungshalle
 6 Congress hall / Kongreßhalle
Business center / Geschäftsviertel
 7 Offices / Büros
 8 Cinema / Kino
 9 Theater
10 Shops / Läden
11 Restaurants and cafés / Restaurants und Cafés
Residential area / Wohnviertel
12 Apartment houses / Apartment-Häuser
13 Elementary school / Grundschule
14 Kindergarten
15 Health center / Gesundheitszentrum
16 Clubhouse / Klubhaus
17 Swimming pool / Schwimmbecken
18 North-south road / Nord-Süd-Straße
19 Parking areas / Parkplätze
20 Santo Antonio monastery / Kloster Santo Antonio
21 Aqueduct / Aquädukt

View of a model of the new city center. ▷
Modellansicht des neuen Stadtzentrums.

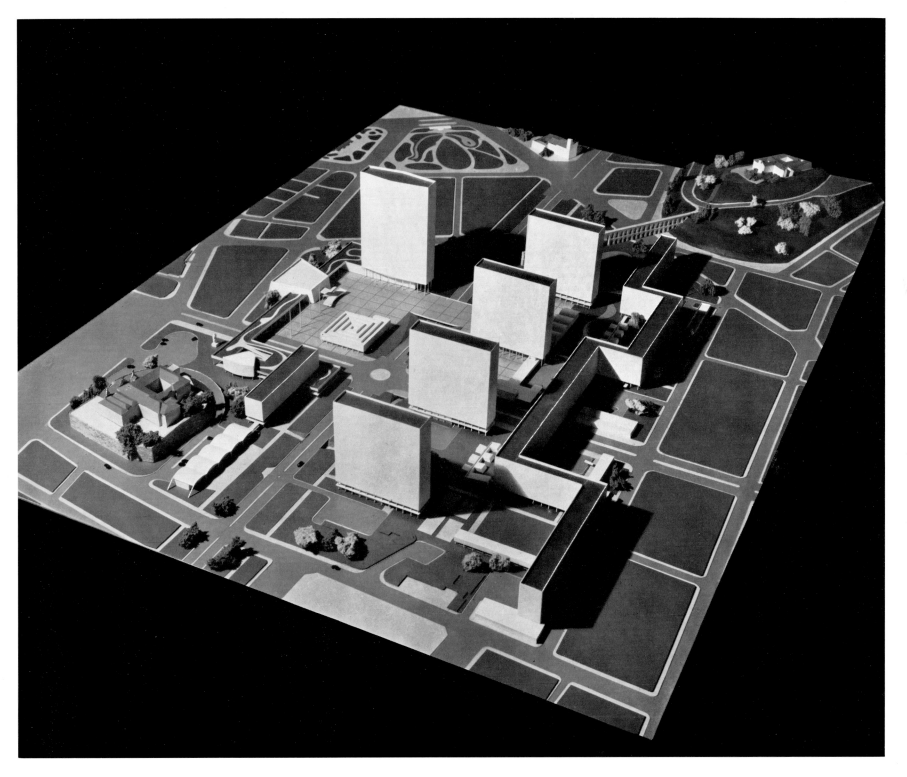

The aqueduct, which is to be preserved as a monument, and part of
the Santo Antonio hill.
Der als Baudenkmal zu erhaltende Aquädukt und ein Teil des Santo-
Antonio-Hügels.

Photo of model: view looking in the same general direction. ▷
Modellfoto: Ansicht mit etwa gleicher Blickrichtung.

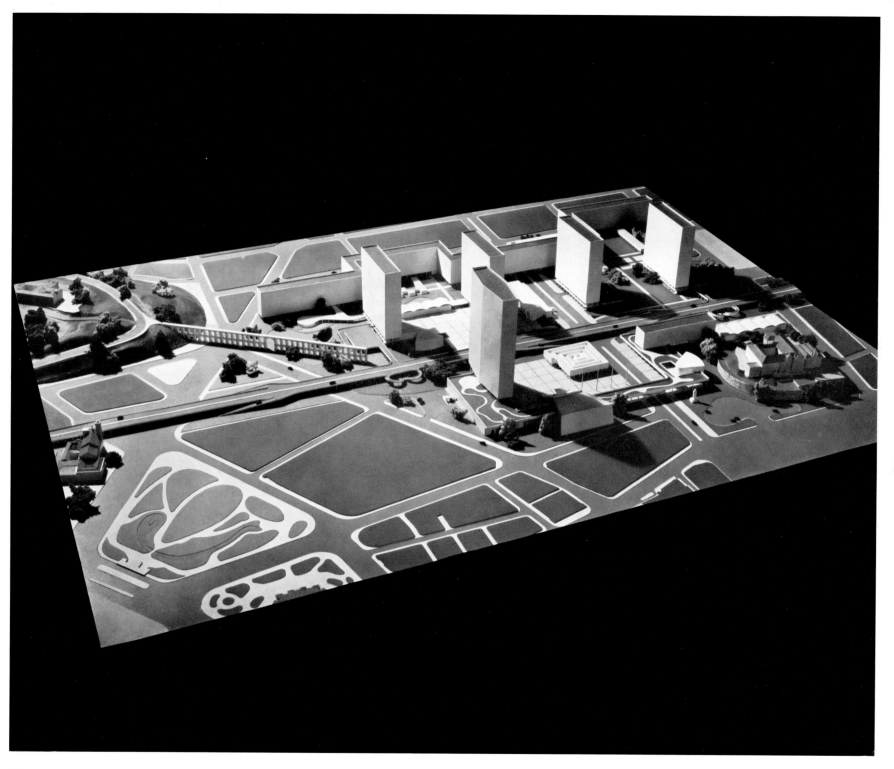

Santo Antonio hill. Wooden huts like those which cover many of the hillsides inside the city area. Part of the hill has already been removed. The earth is used to fill in the coastal strip.
Santo-Antonio-Hügel. Bretterhütten, wie sie viele Hänge innerhalb des Stadtgebietes bedecken. Ein Teil des Hügels ist bereits abgetragen. Die Erde wird zum Aufschütten des Küstenstreifens verwendet.

Photo of model: view looking in the same general direction. ▷
Modellfoto: Ansicht mit etwa gleicher Blickrichtung.

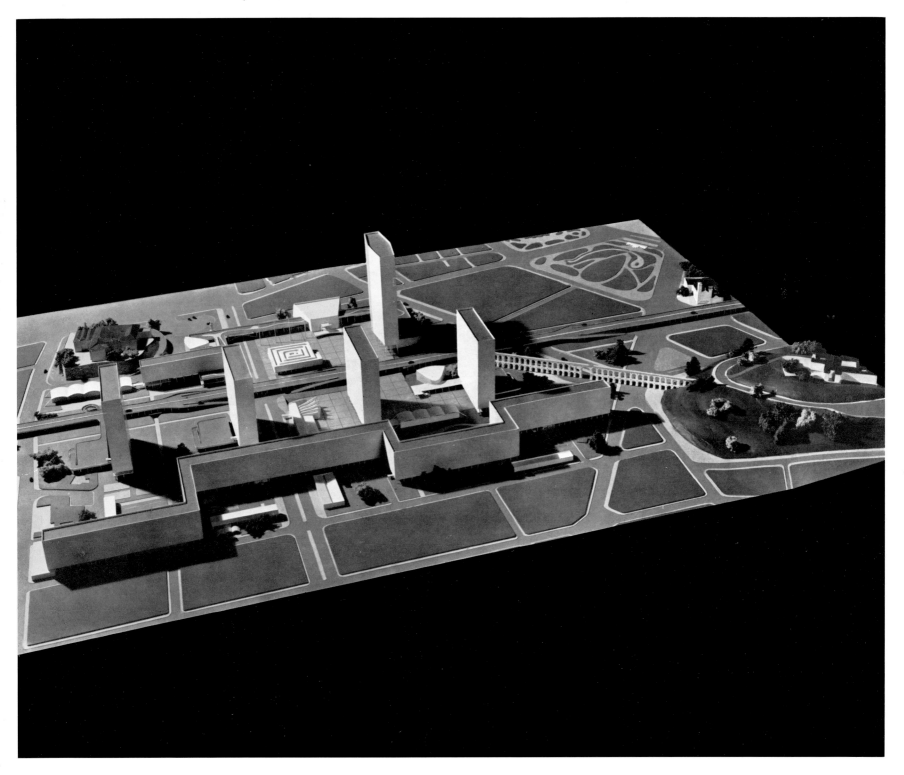

Index of Photographers
Abbildungsnachweis

The numbers following the name indicate the pages on which the photographs are reproduced.
Die angegebenen Nummern beziehen sich auf die Seitenzahlen.